Entrepreneurship
and Small Business Management

Student Activity Workbook

Earl C. Meyer, Ph.D.
Teacher Educator—Marketing Education
Eastern Michigan University
Ypsilanti, Michigan

Kathleen R. Allen, Ph.D.
Assistant Professor of Clinical Entrepreneurship
The Entrepreneur Program
University of Southern California
Los Angeles, California

GLENCOE
McGraw-Hill

New York, New York   Columbus, Ohio   Mission Hills, California   Peoria, Illinois

Send all inquiries to:
GLENCOE/McGraw-Hill
15319 Chatsworth Street
P.O. Box 9609
Mission Hills, CA 91346-9609

ISBN 0-02-675122-4 (Student Activity Workbook)

Printed in the United States of America

5 6 7 8 9 BAW 99 98 97

Table of Contents

Unit Four *Managing and Expanding Your Small Business*

Chapter 1: Our Entrepreneurial Heritage

Name That Entrepreneur

In Chapter 1, you met several entrepreneurs who were important not only to the economic history of the United States but to the social and cultural history as well. Today, there are also entrepreneurs who help shape our economy and have an impact on our social and cultural development.

In this activity, you will identify some modern entrepreneurs. You will also develop your own definition of an entrepreneur and examine how such people affect your life.

1. Based on your reading and experience, what is your definition of an entrepreneur?

   _____

   _____

   _____

   _____

   _____

   _____

   _____

2. Identify three modern entrepreneurs and the nature of their business activity. These can be persons from your community or persons that you have heard or read about elsewhere. You may use library resources, such as magazines and newspapers, to help identify these persons.

   _____

   _____

   _____

   _____

   _____

   _____

   _____

3. Explain your reason(s) for choosing these three entrepreneurs. In your answer, be sure to describe how they are examples of your definition of an entrepreneur.

_____

_____

_____

_____

_____

_____

_____

_____

_____

4. What impact do you think entrepreneurs have on the economy and current business climate? Is it positive or negative? Explain.

_____

_____

_____

_____

_____

_____

_____

_____

_____

_____

_____

Chapter 2: Economic Forces

Elastic or Inelastic?

For each of the following products, indicate if demand would be elastic or inelastic. Explain why.

1. Concert tickets

_____

_____

_____

_____

2. Clothes

_____

_____

_____

3. Shampoo

_____

_____

_____

4. Pizza

_____

_____

_____

5. CDs

_____

_____

_____

6. Toilet paper

_____

_____

_____

_____

7. Stamps

_____

_____

_____

_____

8. Toothpaste

_____

_____

_____

_____

9. Books (other than textbooks) and magazines

_____

_____

_____

_____

10. Local telephone calls

_____

_____

_____

_____

Chapter 2: Economic Forces

More Than You Ever Wanted to Know About Pizza!

You are going to open a pizza delivery business. Your clients will be able to call in an order for a quick, delicious pizza to be delivered to their door. (No eat-in service will be provided.)

Before you begin, you must identify the factors of production required to operate such a business. (Remember that these are the *resources* used by a business.) Using the four factors discussed in the chapter as organizational categories, identify all the needed items you can think of. *Hint:* Interview the owner of a pizza delivery business if you get stumped.

1. Land/Natural Resources

_____   _____

_____   _____

_____   _____

_____   _____

_____   _____

_____   _____

_____   _____

2. Labor

_____   _____

_____   _____

_____   _____

_____   _____

_____   _____

_____   _____

_____   _____

3. Capital

_____   _____

_____   _____

_____   _____

_____   _____

_____   _____

_____   _____

_____   _____

_____   _____

_____   _____

4. Entrepreneurship

_____   _____

_____   _____

_____   _____

_____   _____

_____   _____

_____   _____

_____   _____

_____   _____

_____   _____

Chapter 3: Your Potential as an Entrepreneur

Your Entrepreneurial Experiences

Developing your entrepreneurial potential is often as simple as looking inside yourself. Using the categories mentioned below as a guide, list as many entrepreneurial experiences as you can from your everyday life. A few examples are provided to help you get started.

Classes
- Learning how to post journal entries in business class
- Making oral presentations in English class
- Learning how to calculate percentages in math class

_____

_____

_____

_____

_____

_____

_____

_____

Jobs—Informal
- Pricing according to the competition when mowing lawns

_____

_____

_____

_____

_____

_____

_____

School Organizations

_____

_____

_____

_____

_____

_____

_____

Hobbies
- Reading the business section of the newspaper

_____

_____

_____

_____

_____

_____

Family/Home
- Balancing my checkbook

_____

_____

_____

_____

_____

_____

_____

_____

Traveling

_____

_____

_____

_____

_____

_____

_____

_____

Jobs—Formal
- Calculating markdown before a sale
- Taking inventory
- Doing my taxes

_____

_____

_____

_____

_____

_____

_____

_____

_____

_____

Chapter 3: Your Potential as an Entrepreneur

Creating an Entrepreneurial Profile

The purpose of this activity is to help you understand what makes entrepreneurs tick. By talking with some representative entrepreneurs from your community and comparing their responses, you will be able to develop a profile of entrepreneurs that will assist you as you begin your own entrepreneurial journey.

This activity has three parts. You will need extra paper to record the answers to your interview questions.

A. Interview 2–3 entrepreneurs to find out about the characteristics, motivations, and experiences that have led to their success. Use the following list of questions as a guide for conducting your interviews. *Note:* The interviews may be conducted in person or by telephone.

1. Why did you decide to start your business?

2. Was there a particular incident that led to your decision to start a business?

3. What persons influenced you as you developed your business?

4. How did you decide to start this particular type of business? Where and how did you develop the expertise or the idea for this particular business?

5. What is your educational background?

6. What educational experiences helped you to be more successful?

7. Where and how did you learn the skills you needed to become successful?

8. What is your primary motivation?

9. What personal characteristics do you possess that contribute most to your success?

10. What personal characteristics that you do not now possess would enable you to be more successful, productive, and/or efficient?

11. What are the personal advantages to you of owning your own business?

12. What is the most exciting aspect of owning your own business?

13. What barriers did you overcome in starting your business?

14. Do the advantages of owning your own business outweigh the disadvantages? Please explain.

B. After you interview the entrepreneurs, compare their responses.
Make a list of the common characteristics, motivations, and experiences
they share.

_____   _____

_____   _____

_____   _____

_____   _____

_____   _____

C. Compare your own characteristics, motivations, and experiences
to those you have uncovered. Answer the following questions:

1. What motivates you?

_____

_____

_____

2. Looking back at the earlier activity when you identified your own
entrepreneurial experiences, what do you have in common with
these entrepreneurs?

_____

_____

_____

3. Examine the personal characteristics that the entrepreneurs
identified as contributing to their success. Identify one of these,
and explain how you exhibit this characteristic.

_____

_____

_____

4. Brainstorm a list of ideas that will help you develop your own set of
entrepreneurial characteristics.

_____   _____

_____   _____

_____   _____

Name _____ Date _____

What's Your Potential?

Do you possess any of the distinctive traits that are commonly shared by entrepreneurs? This two-part exercise will help you examine your own potential to become an entrepreneur. It will also help you think about ways to develop your entrepreneurial potential.

A. Listed below are the characteristics or distinctive traits needed to set up an owner-operated business and run it successfully. For each of the traits listed, rank yourself, showing if this trait is most like you or least like you. If you fall somewhere in between, circle the number that you feel is the best indicator.

Characteristic	Most Like Me				Least Like Me
1. Persistent	5	4	3	2	1
2. Creative	5	4	3	2	1
3. Responsible	5	4	3	2	1
4. Inquisitive	5	4	3	2	1
5. Goal-oriented	5	4	3	2	1
6. Independent	5	4	3	2	1
7. Demanding	5	4	3	2	1
8. Self-confident	5	4	3	2	1
9. Risk-taking	5	4	3	2	1
10. Restless	5	4	3	2	1

B. This part of the exercise will help you identify areas where you may need to seek out experiences to improve your entrepreneurial potential. Consider the way you rated yourself on the previous page. As you do, answer the following questions about your entrepreneurial potential. And if your answers are not what you think they should be or what you would wish them to be, remember the words of Al Shapero: "Entrepreneurs are not born. They *become* through learning and life experiences."

1. What have you learned about yourself from filling out the chart on the previous page?

_____

_____

_____

_____

2. What are your strengths?

_____

_____

_____

_____

3. What are your weaknesses?

_____

_____

_____

_____

4. List the categories in which you ranked yourself 3 or lower. For each of these, identify experiences, activities, and ways in which you could improve your entrepreneurial potential.

_____

_____

_____

_____

Name _____   Date _____

Communicating Around the World

Can't speak the language? Don't always count on body language and gestures to communicate your intended message accurately. Below is a list of gestures that are common in the United States. Read the description of each, and in the second column of the chart briefly explain what it means in this country.

An alternate meaning for another country is also given. Imagine how confusing your message might be if you used the same gesture there!

Gesture	Meaning in the United States	Meaning in Other Countries
1. Head nod	_____	In Bulgaria and Greece, signifies no.
2. V sign, palm out	_____ _____	In most of Europe, means victory.
3. Circle created by touching thumb and forefinger	_____ _____ _____	In Greece, may create enemies as it is considered impolite. In southern France, means "zero" or "worthless."
4. Crossed fingers	_____ _____	In Europe, means "protection" or "good luck." In Paraguay, may be offensive.
5. Thumbs up	_____ _____	In Australia, a very rude gesture.
6. Circular motion of the finger around the ear	_____ _____	In the Netherlands, if someone gives you this signal, means you have a phone call.
7. Waving the whole hand back and forth in someone's face	_____ _____ _____	In Greece, a serious insult. The closer to the person's face, the more threatening the gesture is considered.
8. Arms folded across your chest	_____ _____ _____	In Finland, means you are arrogant or proud. In Fiji, shows disrespect.

Entrepreneurship and Small Business Management

Chapter 4: Business Communication

All Ears?

To complete this activity, you must find a partner. Ask your partner first to read aloud the portion of the interview with Body Shop founder Anita Roddick that appears below. Then have your reader ask questions 1–6 on the next page. You should answer the questions in writing *without* looking back at the text. Check your answers, and then go on to the final stage of the activity.

"What is The Body Shop?"

"We make and sell our own naturally-based products which cleanse, polish, and protect the skin and hair.

"This is The Body Shop in a nutshell. But it's by no means the whole story.

"I started The Body Shop in Brighton, England, in 1976. There are now over 600 branches of The Body Shop in 40 countries from Norway to New Zealand. We're trading in 20 languages, and we're still growing.

"That kind of success always sparks people's curiosity. They want to know how and why. The answer is simple. In fact, it's as simple as the original idea for The Body Shop. It made sense to me to find out what customers wanted, then try and get it for them and sell them as much or as little of it as they felt like buying without all the unnecessary, expensive packaging and hype that people associate with the cosmetics industry. I thought it was important that my business concern itself not just with skin and hair care preparations but also with the community, the environment, and the big wide world beyond cosmetics.

"I believe that from the very beginning we tapped into a common thread of humanity. Simplicity has a lot of appeal in an increasingly complex world. So does honesty. That's why our customers cut across all boundaries of age, gender, and nationality. What they all have in common is that they want to know the story behind what they buy. And The Body Shop has many stories to tell, because the ideas and the ingredients for our formulations come from such a rich variety of sources— everything from folkloric recipes that have been tried and tested by human beings for thousands of years to tips harvested by our visits to tribal cultures around the globe. I don't think The Body Shop will ever lose the sense of adventure that is attached to the pursuit of knowledge."

From Body Shop promotional literature.

1. What is The Body Shop?

_____

_____

_____

2. When was The Body Shop founded?

_____

3. How many branches of The Body Shop are there?

_____

4. The Body Shop has branches in how many countries?

_____

5. What is the source of The Body Shop's ingredients and formulas?

_____

_____

6. Who are The Body Shop's primary customers?

_____

_____

Now that you have answered the specific questions about The Body Shop,
review the text and see how well you listened.

7. What are some techniques you can use to improve your listening skills?

_____   _____

_____   _____

_____   _____

_____   _____

_____   _____

Chapter 4: Business Communication

Assessing Your Self-disclosure

Chapter 4 emphasizes the need for effective communication in business. Effective communication involves three elements—the message (what is being communicated), the receiver (who is receiving the message), and the medium (how the message is being sent). When you are the medium, the one sending the message, you must realize that how you deliver it can be as important as the message itself. Does the receiver believe you are to be trusted, that you care about him or her, and that you have heard what he or she is saying? These issues will have a significant impact on how the message is received and, perhaps, on your success as a businessperson.

Sending the right message includes sending the right message about yourself. This is self-disclosure—how you present yourself and form some bond with the other person. The following exercise will show you how you disclose yourself to significant people in your life. It will help you see how you disclose or present yourself to others. Complete this exercise and answer the questions that follow.

Choose the five or six most important people in your life. These could include your mother, father, guardian, brother, sister, grandparent (or other relative), best friend, boyfriend, or girlfriend. Then read each item in the chart that appears on pages 17 and 18. In the columns at the right, indicate the degree to which you have discussed the subject with each of the people you selected. Use the following rating scale:

0	Have told the other person nothing about this aspect of me.
1	Have talked in general terms about this. The other person knows some of the facts but not the complete message.
2	Have told the other person about this completely, including my observations, thoughts, feelings, and needs.
X	Have lied or misrepresented myself regarding this aspect. The other person has a false picture of me.

	Mother or Guardian	Father or Guardian	Brother/Sister	Grandparents or Other Relative	Best Friend	Boyfriend or Girlfriend

Tastes and Interests

1. My favorite (and least favorite) foods and beverages ....
2. My likes and dislikes in music...........
3. My favorite reading material ....
4. The kinds of movies and TV shows I like ....
5. The style of house and the kinds of furnishings I like best.......................
6. The kind of party or social gathering I like best ....

Attitudes and Opinions

1. What I think and feel about religion.
2. My views on racial integration in schools ....
3. My personal views on alcohol and drugs ....
4. My personal views on sexual morality
5. My personal standards of attractiveness in men or women.....................
6. The things I regard as desirable for a man to be ....
7. The things I regard as desirable for a woman to be ....

Work and Studies

1. Type of work/class I enjoy most ....
2. Type of work/class I enjoy least........
3. What I feel are my shortcomings and handicaps as a worker/student ....
4. What I feel are my strong points as a worker/student...............................
5. How I feel my work is appreciated by others ....
6. My ambitions and goals....................

Name _____ Date _____

	Mother or Guardian	Father or Guardian	Brother/Sister	Grandparents or Other Relative	Best Friend	Boyfriend or Girlfriend

Money

1. How much money I make at work or get as an allowance.....................

2. Whether or not I owe money. If so, how much and to whom ....

3. Whether or not I have savings and the amount...............................

4. Whether or not others owe me money, the amount, and who owes it to me.....

5. Whether or not I gamble and how much ....

6. All of my present sources of income ....

Personality

1. The aspects of my personality that I dislike.................................

2. The feelings I have trouble expressing or controlling ....

3. Whether or not I feel I am attractive to the opposite sex ....

4. Things in the past or present I feel ashamed or guilty about...................

5. What I fear most................................

Body

1. My feelings about the appearance of my face................................

2. My feelings about the appearance of the rest of my body.......................

3. How I wished I looked.....................

4. Whether or not I have any health problems ....

5. My past record of illness and treatment................................

6. Whether or not I make a special effort to keep fit, healthy, and attractive.....

Adapted from *Messages: The Communication Skills Book* by McKay, Davis, and Fanning. Copyright © 1985 by New Harbinger Publications.

1. What did you learn about your self-disclosure? For example, how does the closeness of the relationship affect disclosure? Did you have many X's? How do you explain this?

_____

_____

_____

_____

_____

_____

_____

_____

_____

_____

2. Based on this exercise, how do you feel you present yourself as a person? Do you believe this would have any effect on your success in business? Explain.

_____

_____

_____

_____

_____

_____

_____

_____

_____

_____

_____

Entrepreneurship and Small Business Management

3. Think of stores you frequent. Describe the traits, demeanor, and attitude of the personnel in them. Do you think their personalities affect your attitude about supporting the business? Explain.

_____

_____

_____

_____

_____

_____

_____

_____

_____

_____

_____

Name _____ Date _____

Chapter 5: Math for Entrepreneurs

Verify the Opening Cash Fund

Practice makes perfect! As you learned from this chapter, accuracy is very important when operating a cash register. If the opening cash fund is not correct, it will lead to errors in sales which are reported at the end of the day.

Your job is to make sure that the opening cash fund is correct. For each situation identified below, calculate the dollar amounts and totals for the opening cash fund. If the amount in your cash fund is balanced, or equal to the amount it should be, circle *Balanced*. If it is less than it should be, circle *Under*. If it is more than it should be, circle *Over*. *Note:* A roll of pennies is worth $.50; nickels, $2.00; dimes, $5.00; and quarters, $10.00.

1. Your opening cash fund should be $100. You find the following coins and bills in the cash drawer:

   3 rolls of pennies   _____

   2 rolls of nickels   _____

   5 rolls of dimes   _____

   2 rolls of quarters   _____

   10 one-dollar bills   _____

   2 five-dollar bills   _____

   3 ten-dollar bills   _____

   TOTAL   _____   Balanced   Over   Under

2. Your opening cash fund should be $50. You find the following coins and bills in the cash drawer:

   2 rolls of pennies   _____

   2 rolls of nickels   _____

   1 roll of dimes   _____

   1 roll of quarters   _____

   20 one-dollar bills   _____

   2 five-dollar bills   _____

   TOTAL   _____   Balanced   Over   Under

3. Your opening cash fund should be $75. You find the following coins and bills in the cash drawer:

4 rolls of pennies	_____
1 roll of nickels	_____
1 roll of dimes	_____
1 roll of quarters	_____
20 one-dollar bills	_____
5 five-dollar bills	_____
1 ten-dollar bill	_____
TOTAL	_____ Balanced Over Under

4. Your opening cash fund should be $100. You find the following coins and bills in the cash drawer:

2 rolls of pennies	_____
2 rolls of nickels	_____
2 rolls of dimes	_____
1 roll of quarters	_____
25 one-dollar bills	_____
4 five-dollar bills	_____
1 ten-dollar bill	_____
1 twenty-dollar bill	_____
TOTAL	_____ Balanced Over Under

Name _____ Date _____

The Great Balancing Act!

At the end of each business day, the cash drawer should be balanced. For each situation given below, calculate the total receipts for the day and determine the actual cash receipts in the drawer. If the amount of money and checks in the cash drawer is equal to the amount that appears on the register tape, circle *Balanced*. If it is less than it should be, circle *Under* and state the amount under. If it is more than it should be, circle *Over* and state the amount over.

1. Your register tape shows receipts of $1,201.35. You count up the drawer's contents and arrive at these figures:

Cash	$ 453.23
Checks	371.07
Credit sales	516.05
Total receipts	$ _____
Cash refunds	63.00
Adjusted receipts	$ _____
Opening cash fund	75.00
Actual receipts	$ _____

   Over   Balanced   Under $ _____

2. Your register tape shows receipts of $745.00. You count up the drawer's contents and arrive at these figures:

Cash	$ 249.27
Checks	450.25
Credit sales	115.97
Total receipts	$ _____
Cash refunds	25.49
Adjusted receipts	$ _____
Opening cash fund	50.00
Actual receipts	$ _____

   Over   Balanced   Under $ _____

Entrepreneurship and Small Business Management   **23**

3. Your register tape shows receipts of $2,125.00. You count up the drawer's contents and arrive at these figures:

Cash	$ 340.00
Checks	745.00
Credit sales	1,200.00
Total receipts	$ _____
Cash refunds	85.00
Adjusted receipts	$ _____
Opening cash fund	75.00
Actual receipts	$ _____

    Over   Balanced   Under $ _____

4. Your register tape shows receipts of $2,728.14. You count up the drawer's contents and arrive at these figures:

Cash	$ 654.14
Checks	999.68
Credit sales	1,287.32
Total receipts	$ _____
Cash refunds	113.00
Adjusted receipts	$ _____
Opening cash fund	100.00
Actual receipts	$ _____

    Over   Balanced   Under $ _____

5. Your register tape shows receipts of $710.83. You count up the drawer's contents and arrive at these figures:

Cash	$ 471.54
Checks	281.29
Credit sales	0.00
Total receipts	$ _____
Cash refunds	0.00
Adjusted receipts	$ _____
Opening cash fund	50.00
Actual receipts	$ _____

    Over   Balanced   Under $ _____

Chapter 5: Math for Entrepreneurs

Coffees from Around the World

Many times an entrepreneur is required to perform several math calculations in order to complete a sale. On the next two pages is an order form from a gourmet coffee shop. Based on the information given, complete the calculations and successfully carry out the sale.

The transaction is a phone order that the customer wants shipped as a gift. The shipping and handling charges should be calculated on the basis of ground service.

Stauf's
Coffee Roasters
1277 Grandview Ave., Columbus, Ohio 43212

- ♥ Full bodied
- ♥ Medium bodied
- ♡ Light bodied

Coffees

AFRICAN AND ASIAN	No. of LBS.	Price/ LB.	Total
♥ Tanzanian Peaberry		6.75	
♥ Kenya AA		6.95	
♥ Zimbabwe 053		7.50	
♥ Ethiopian Mocca Harrar		6.95	
♥ Ethiopian Sidamo Yergecheffe		7.50	
♥ Indian Malabar	1	8.25	
♥ Yemen Mattari	1	11.75	

PRIVATE GOURMET BLENDS & SPECIAL ROASTS	No. of LBS.	Price/ LB.	Total
♡ Mid Morning Blend		5.95	
♥ Breakfast Blend		6.25	
♥ Stauf's House Blend	3	6.25	
♥ Mocca Java Blend		6.75	
♥ Evening Blend		5.95	
♥ Kaldi's Blend		5.95	
♥ Vienna Roast		6.00	
♥ French Roast	2	6.25	
♥ Stauf's Espresso Blend		6.50	

DECAFFEINATED COFFEES (SWISS WATER PROCESS)	No. of LBS.	Price/ LB.	Total
♥ Colombian Excelso		8.95	
♥ Guatemalan Antigua		9.50	
♥ Kenya AA		9.75	
♥ Mexican Pluma Altura		7.95	
♥ Stauf's House Blend		9.25	
♥ Mocca Java Blend		9.75	
♥ Ethiopian Mocca Harrar		9.75	
♥ Sumatra Lintong		9.75	
♥ Java Timor Estate		9.75	
♥ Costa Rican Tarazu'		8.95	
♥ Evening Blend		8.95	
♥ Kaldi's Blend	2	8.50	
♥ Italian Roast	1	9.25	

FLAVORED COFFEES	No. of LBS.	Price/ LB.	Total
Amaretto	1/2	6.50	
Chocolate		6.50	
Chocolate Hazelnut	1/2	6.50	
Chocolate Irish Cream		6.50	
Chocolate Mint		6.50	
Cinnamon	1	6.50	
Hazelnut		6.50	
Irish Cream		6.50	
Macadamia Nut Cream		6.50	
Vanilla Almond		6.50	
Vanilla Hazelnut		6.50	

DECAFFEINATED FLAVORED COFFEES (SWISS WATER PROCESS)	No. of LBS.	Price/ LB.	Total
Amaretto		9.50	
Chocolate		9.50	
Chocolate Hazelnut		9.50	
Chocolate Irish Cream		9.50	
Chocolate Mint		9.50	
Cinnamon		9.50	
Hazelnut	1	9.50	
Irish Cream		9.50	
Macadamia Nut Cream		9.50	
Vanilla Almond		9.50	
Vanilla Hazelnut		9.50	

Stauf's
Coffee Roasters
Instructions

MAIL ORDER

GRINDING METHODS:

☒ *Whole Bean* ☐ *Percolator* ☐ *Manual Drip*
☐ *Auto Drip* ☐ *Fine* ☐ *Espresso*
☐ *Other*

COFFEE TOTAL $ _____
SHIPPING (see tables) $ _____
TOTAL Amount $ _____

☐ Check   ☐ Money Order   ☒ Visa   ☐ Mastercard

Expiration Date: _____ 6/96 _____

| 1 | 2 | 3 | 4 | 5 | 6 | 7 | 8 | 9 | 0 | | | | | | |

- Phone orders gladly taken with valid Visa/Mastercard
- Checks/Money Orders payable to Stauf's Coffee Roasters

SHIP TO:

NAME *Jason Koryaski*
ADDRESS *5182 Sunset Blvd.*

CITY *Los Angeles*
STATE/ZIP *CA   90046*
DAYTIME PHONE # (*818*) *555-1212*

FROM:

NAME *Andrea Rollins*
ADDRESS *5283 S. 3rd St.*

CITY *Columbus*
STATE/ZIP *OH   43206*
DAYTIME PHONE # (*614*) *258-5040*

SHIPPING & HANDLING CHARGES

GROUND SERVICE

ZONE	2	3	4	5	6	7	8
Lbs.							
2	2.45	2.55	2.85	2.95	3.10	3.25	3.45
3	2.50	2.65	3.00	3.20	3.40	3.60	3.85
4	2.60	2.80	3.15	3.35	3.65	3.95	4.25
5	2.70	2.90	3.30	3.50	3.85	4.25	4.60
6	2.80	3.00	3.40	3.70	4.10	4.50	4.95
7	2.85	3.10	3.55	3.90	4.35	4.85	5.35
8	2.95	3.25	3.75	4.10	4.65	5.20	5.75
9	3.05	3.35	3.90	4.30	4.95	5.55	6.15
10	3.15	3.45	4.05	4.55	5.20	5.90	6.60
11	3.25	3.60	4.25	4.75	5.45	6.25	7.00
12	3.30	3.75	4.40	4.95	5.75	6.75	7.45

Over **12** lbs. add

.15/lb.   .25/lb.   .40/lb.

2ND DAY AIR SERVICE

Lbs.	48 States	Alaska & Hawaii
2	5.00	7.50
3	6.00	8.50
4	7.00	10.00
5	7.50	11.00
6	8.50	12.50
7	9.50	13.50
8	10.50	15.00
9	11.50	16.00
10	12.50	17.50
11	13.50	18.50
12	14.50	19.50
Over **12** lbs. add	1.00/lb.	1.25/lb.

GROUND ZONES

To determine your zone, locate the first 3 digits of your ZIP code on the chart. Your corresponding zone number is on the right. The shipping charge is determined by your zone and the weight of your order.

ZIP	ZONE	ZIP	ZONE	ZIP	ZONE
004-005	4	300-315	4	577	6
010-013	4	316	5	580-585	5
014-033	5	317-319	4	586-593	6
034	4	320-339	5	594-599	7
035	5	342-349	5	600-609	3
036	4	350-364	4	610-616	4
037-050	5	365-366	5	617-619	3
051-054	4	367-369	4	620-623	4
055-056	5	370-372	3	624	3
057	4	373-375	4	625-647	4
058-059	5	376-379	3	648	5
060-089	4	380-384	4	649-663	4
100-139	4	385	3	664-692	5
140-143	3	386	4	693	6
144-146	4	387	5	700-719	5
147	3	388-389	4	720-726	4
148-149	4	390-392	5	727-732	5
150-153	2	393	4	733	6
154-168	3	394-396	5	734-767	5
169-199	4	397-399	4	768-769	6
200-214	4	400-406	2	770-778	5
215	3	407-409	3	779-791	6
216-225	4	410-414	2	792	5
226-229	3	415-418	3	793-799	6
230-238	4	420	4	800-838	6
239-249	3	421-427	3	831-864	7
250-253	2	430-462	2	865-885	6
254	3	463-466	3	889-893	7
255-257	2	467-473	2	894-897	8
258-259	3	474-495	3	898	7
260-261	2	496-499	4	900-961	8
262	3	500-509	4	970-978	7
263-264	2	510-516	5	979	7
265	3	520-533	4	980-986	8
266	2	534	3	988-989	8
267-274	3	535-555	4	990-992	7
275-285	4	556-558	5	993	8
286-289	3	559	4	994	7
290-299	4	560-576	5		

Used by permission of Stauf's Coffee Roasters.

Chapter 5: Math for Entrepreneurs

What's My Extension?

How would you like to be billed for more merchandise than you ordered? Or worse yet, how would you like to be billed for merchandise that hasn't even been shipped?

The invoice that appears on this page requires you to calculate extensions (multiple the quantity ordered by the unit price) in order to total the invoice. After you finish this, there is another challenge waiting for you on the next page!

Invoice 1001

CUSTOMER NO.   61432

SOLD TO: Ray's Specialty Foods   SHIP TO: Same
125 High Street
Charleston, WV 25312

DATE	SHIP VIA	F.O.B.	TERMS
1/17	UPS		2/10, net 30

PURCHASE ORDER NUMBER		ORDER DATE	SALESPERSON	OUR ORDER NUMBER
12574		1/15	CRC	

QTY. ORDERED	QTY. SHIPPED	QTY. B.O.	ITEM NUMBER	DESCRIPTION	UNIT PRICE	EXTENDED PRICE
2	2		3245	Bread Display Rack	45.00	
1	1		3276	Aluminum Baking Rack	30.00	
7	7		3255	Case / Olive Oil	67.00	
					Subtotal	
					Tax (5%)	
					Shipping	15.00
					Total	

Thank You for Your Business

As a rule, businesses do not invoice customers for goods until those goods are actually shipped. The invoice that appears on this page contains some items that are on back order. (In other words, they are not available for shipment.) Calculate the extensions and totals, taking the general rule into account. *Hint:* Give special attention to the Quantity Shipped column in totaling the invoice.

Invoice 1002

CUSTOMER NO.   52415

SOLD TO: Denver Public Schools
1234 Rocky Mountain Way
Denver, CO 30345

SHIP TO: Attention Purchasing

DATE	SHIP VIA	F.O.B.	TERMS
3/15			2/10, net 30

PURCHASE ORDER NUMBER	ORDER DATE	SALESPERSON	OUR ORDER NUMBER
52312	3/10	PPM	2523

QTY. ORDERED	QTY. SHIPPED	QTY. B.O.	ITEM NUMBER	DESCRIPTION	UNIT PRICE	EXTENDED PRICE
5	3	2	13245		20.00	
4	0	4	32512		25.00	
1	1	0	25333		27.00	
3	2	1	32521		45.00	
					Subtotal	
					Shipping	7.00
					Total	

Thank You for Your Business

Chapter 6: Decision Skills

Goal Setting

Listed below and on the next page are five business situations that incorporate goal statements. (In each case, the goal statement appears in bold type.) Identify what, if anything, is wrong with the goals as stated, based on what you learned in this chapter. Then write an improved version.

1. Marta Vargo is the owner of an athletic store specializing in clothing and shoes for runners. When asked what her goal for the business is, she said, **"I want to increase sales."**

_____

_____

_____

_____

_____

_____

_____

2. Lester Dawson operates an auto detailing service. Business has increased so rapidly that he doesn't have enough help. **Lester's goal is to hire additional workers by January.** How can you help Lester with this goal?

_____

_____

_____

_____

_____

_____

_____

3. Emilo Sanchez runs a local transportation company. He has experienced a noticeable reduction in customers. The reason seems to be that deliveries are not being made on time. **His goal is to show an increase of 20 percent in three months.**

_____

_____

_____

_____

_____

_____

4. Lucinda Spears sells imported Persian rugs to retail outlets. Because of political unrest in the country from which she has been importing rugs, she has been trying to find other suppliers. As a result of problems with untested suppliers, however, her inventory has decreased by 30 percent. **Lucinda wants to increase suppliers and rugs by 20 percent.**

_____

_____

_____

_____

_____

_____

5. Jen Hawkins is an antique dealer in a small, rural community. She wants to expand her customer base. She currently has a 5 percent share of the market and wants to increase that. **Her goal is to capture 20 percent of the market in the next three months.**

_____

_____

_____

_____

_____

_____

Chapter 6: Decision Skills

Flowers for Frieda: an Exercise in Decision Making

Entrepreneurs in all areas of business are faced with numerous decisions every day. In many cases, their success depends on how well they examine a situation and make those decisions. Your success with this activity will depend on how well you analyze the information given below, using the steps in the formal decision-making process.

You are the owner of a local flower shop. Two of your business associates are getting married on Saturday, and you have been hired to design the floral arrangements for both weddings. The plans have been finalized for months, and the couples are expecting great things. Orders for some of the flowers were placed weeks ago because several of the flowers being used are grown only in tropical climates and are difficult to obtain.

It is the Monday before the weddings. On the previous Thursday, Hurricane Frieda ripped through the Hawaiian Islands. Your major suppliers of flowers are located on the islands, and you have just received a fax that the current crop of flowers has been destroyed. What might be salvaged is not available for immediate shipment because the airports will be closed for several days. The earliest that you might receive a shipment would be Friday, the day before the weddings.

Your challenge, if you want to maintain the good opinion of your associates and continue in business, is to solve this problem using the steps in formal decision making as outlined below. Try to be creative and realistic as you come up with a solution (or solutions) to address this difficult situation. Space is provided on this and the next two pages for you to work through your decision.

You may need additional sheets of paper to explore your ideas thoroughly. Don't let your creativity be limited by the space provided on the page! Be entrepreneurial as you come up with your solution.

1. **Identify the problem or opportunity.** Based on the information given, state the problem or opportunity as you see it.

_____

_____

_____

_____

_____

_____

_____

2. **List the solutions or options.** List and explain as many possible solutions as you can think of. (Consider contacting a florist if you need help.)

_____

_____

_____

_____

_____

_____

_____

_____

_____

3. **Evaluate the alternatives.** Discuss each alternative, weighing its advantages and disadvantages.

_____

_____

_____

_____

_____

_____

_____

_____

_____

_____

_____

4. **Choose a solution.** Explain the reasons for your choice.

_____

_____

_____

_____

_____

_____

_____

_____

_____

5. **Act and get feedback.** What will you do to carry out your plan to solve the problem? How will you know if you are successful?

_____

_____

_____

_____

_____

_____

_____

_____

_____

Chapter 6: Decision Skills

The Case of the Missing Halloween Lanterns

It is extremely important in the successful operation of a business to clearly communicate your goals and expectations. The following dialogue is an example of the problems that come up when the goals are not clearly communicated.

Read the dialogue below. Keep in mind the steps that ensure that the goals you set will have the best possible chance of being achieved. Then answer the questions that follow.

Mr. Sergeant: Stephanie, when are the Halloween lanterns going to be finished?

Stephanie: I don't know. I didn't know you wanted me to take care of them.

Mr. Sergeant: Remember, I asked you two months ago to put that on your list of things to do.

Stephanie: You mentioned it briefly once. But since you didn't follow up with a memo, I thought you had decided to use someone else.

Mr. Sergeant: But you've always done the lanterns. I assumed you would do them this year.

Stephanie: I know, but at the beginning of the year when we were discussing long-range goals, you talked about giving that responsibility to someone else so I would be more involved with sales.

Mr. Sergeant: Well, we really have a problem now. There are only three months till Halloween, and we need to have the merchandise ready in one month. We have orders that need to be shipped, and this could be a major loss for us.

Stephanie: I don't know what to suggest. Do you have any ideas?

Mr. Sergeant: Perhaps Olivia could free up the time in her schedule to do this.

Stephanie: Do you know what we need so you can tell her exactly what she is facing?

Mr. Sergeant: We need 800 lantern units by the first of September.

Stephanie: Do you think, realistically, she can do it?

Mr. Sergeant: I think so, but I'll need to tell her our goal and see if she thinks she can handle it.

Stephanie: You might want to put it in writing for her. That way she can see exactly what your expectations are and the time line she is working with. Then, I think she would have a better chance of getting the job done.

Mr. Sergeant: That's a good idea. I'll send her a memo right away.

1. What is the problem?

_____

_____

_____

_____

_____

_____

_____

_____

2. Why didn't Stephanie know that she was supposed to make the lanterns?

_____

_____

_____

_____

_____

_____

_____

_____

_____

3. What does Mr. Sergeant need to do to communicate his goals?

_____

_____

_____

_____

_____

_____

4. What is wrong with the goal that Mr. Sergeant finally sets?

_____

_____

_____

_____

_____

_____

_____

5. How would you have communicated the original goal to Stephanie?
Write a clear goal statement.

_____

_____

_____

_____

_____

_____

_____

Chapter 7: Selecting Your Field

Entrepreneurial Alchemy

Alchemy is the ancient practice of trying to turn base metals into gold. Entrepreneurial alchemy, then, might be considered taking the "base metal" of your experience and turning it into the "gold" of a successful business.

So, now it's time for you to practice alchemy. Listed below are seven rather ordinary businesses or products. As the entrepreneurial alchemist, try to list at least five creative ways to turn these ideas into the gold of business success. Have fun unleashing your creativity!

1. Movie theater

   a. _____

   b. _____

   c. _____

   d. _____

   e. _____

2. Jewelry

   a. _____

   b. _____

   c. _____

   d. _____

   e. _____

3. Video store

   a. _____

   b. _____

   c. _____

   d. _____

   e. _____

4. Body care products

    a. _____

    b. _____

    c. _____

    d. _____

    e. _____

5. Sunglasses

    a. _____

    b. _____

    c. _____

    d. _____

    e. _____

6. Catering

    a. _____

    b. _____

    c. _____

    d. _____

    e. _____

7. Fabric store

    a. _____

    b. _____

    c. _____

    d. _____

    e. _____

Name _____   Date _____

The Profit of Experience

Someone once said, "Experience is the best teacher." Likewise, your experience may be your best hope for a successful business.

Chapter 7 discusses how to transform your personal experiences into profitable ideas. The first step, of course, is to understand which experiences you have had that might be valuable.

1. List ten experiences you have had that you think might be transformed into ideas for a business. These can be things you have done, seen, or even dreamed!

    a. _____

    b. _____

    c. _____

    d. _____

    e. _____

    f. _____

    g. _____

    h. _____

    i. _____

    j. _____

2. Now, for each experience listed above, develop one business idea. In other words, state *how* would you transform the experience into a profitable business.

    a. _____

    b. _____

    c. _____

    d. _____

    e. _____

f. _____

g. _____

h. _____

i. _____

j. _____

3. Now comes the real fun. Select *one* of these spectacular ideas, and examine its potential for profit based on the following questions.

   Selected idea: _____

   a. Is this a good idea? (Of course it's a good idea, but how does it meet a need that is not currently being met? Or how can you make it unique?)

   _____

   _____

   _____

   _____

   _____

   _____

   _____

   b. Is this a good idea *for you*? (Is this something you feel you could do or learn to do? More importantly, would you enjoy doing it?)

   _____

   _____

   _____

   _____

   _____

   _____

   _____

c. What is your potential for profit? Who will your customers be?

_____

_____

_____

_____

_____

_____

_____

_____

_____

_____

d. How will you begin?

_____

_____

_____

_____

_____

_____

_____

_____

_____

_____

_____

Chapter 7: Selecting Your Field

Repotting Your Blooming Business

In selecting your field and coming up with a winning idea, you don't have to reinvent the wheel. As you visit other communities and neighborhoods, read books and magazines, look at the newspaper, and watch TV and movies, you are constantly looking at business ideas. Some of these you have never heard of. Others you knew of but certainly never thought of as your future.

"Repotting" is taking a good idea and replanting it in your area and, with your special care and attention, making it grow into a blooming success. This activity is intended to help you expand your awareness of the possibilities that are already within your reach, waiting for you to touch them.

1. List ten businesses that are not currently in existence in your local area. You may wish to recall trips you have made, look in the library, interview friends, watch TV, or create something yourself. If you live in a large city, narrow your scope to your immediate community.

a. _____

b. _____

c. _____

d. _____

e. _____

f. _____

g. _____

h. _____

i. _____

j. _____

Now you have business ideas that you could transplant. Answer the following questions to analyze whether or not each of these businesses could survive in the economic and social climate of your community.

2. Is this business good for your community? Why or why not?

a. _____

_____

b. _____

_____

c. _____

_____

d. _____

_____

e. _____

_____

f. _____

_____

g. _____

_____

h. _____

_____

i. _____

_____

j. _____

_____

3. Select two of the businesses that you analyzed in the previous question. Why would these businesses be good for you?

    Selected business: _____

_____

_____

_____

_____

    Selected business: _____

_____

_____

_____

_____

_____

4. Who will be your customers?

    Selected business: _____

_____

_____

_____

_____

    Selected business: _____

_____

_____

_____

_____

Chapter 8: Types of Business Ownership

The Ownership Match

Select a type of business that you may want to start based on the exploration you did in Chapter 7. (*Hint:* You may want to look back at the activities from Chapter 7 to select a business.) Then use the chart and follow the steps below. A sample, using restaurants as the type of business, is given to help you get started.

- Think of the businesses in your area that are the type you may want start. List four of them.
- Identify the type of ownership for each business that you list. (This may require some research.)
- For each business, list an advantage and disadvantage for the particular form of ownership.

Type of business: _____

Name of Business	Form of Ownership	Advantage of Form of Ownership for this Business	Disadvantage of Form of Ownership for this Business
Example: Max & Mabel's	Corporation	Easier to raise money	Fees and restrictions
1.			
2.			
3.			
4.			

Chapter 8: Types of Business Ownership

Edna and Elmer Carving Up a Tree

Elmer and Edna had known each other for a long time. Edna wanted to open a store featuring original wood carvings. She also wanted to sell tools and other carving products. She knew that Elmer was a good wood carver, but he didn't care much for business. However, Elmer had the resources needed to begin such a business. With Edna's business sense, knowledge of the field, and enthusiasm, she knew she could make it work. All she needed was Elmer's interest in wood carving, his contacts with other carvers, and his financial resources.

When Edna approached Elmer with the idea, he was interested but a little skeptical. She had suggested that he become a limited partner so he wouldn't have to be involved with running the business. Elmer wanted more. He wanted a full partnership, with its shared responsibility for decision making. They seemed to be at odds until Edna presented a solution.

1. Why do you think Elmer was not happy when Edna suggested that he become a limited partner?

_____

_____

_____

_____

_____

_____

2. What do you think Edna's solution was? *Hint:* Refer to Chapter 8, and review the elements that lead to the greatest potential for partnership success.

_____

_____

_____

_____

_____

_____

3. You are now Edna and Elmer's attorney. They have asked you to draw up a partnership agreement for them. Using the headings that appear on this and the following three pages as a guide, develop a partnership agreement that you believe Edna and Elmer would sign. You will need to use your imagination in developing this contract.

Name of Business

_____

_____

Purpose

_____

_____

_____

_____

Duration of Agreement

_____

_____

Character of Partners (general or limited, active or silent)

_____

_____

_____

_____

Businesses Expenses (how handled)

_____

_____

_____

_____

_____

Division of Profits and Losses

_____

_____

_____

_____

_____

_____

_____

Salaries

_____

_____

_____

_____

_____

_____

_____

Death of a Partner

_____

_____

_____

_____

_____

_____

_____

_____

Handling of Business Disagreements

_____

_____

_____

_____

_____

_____

_____

_____

_____

_____

Responsibilities of Partners

_____

_____

_____

_____

_____

_____

_____

_____

_____

_____

_____

_____

_____

Entrepreneurship and Small Business Management   **49**

Other Additions (anything else that you think should be included)

_____

_____

_____

_____

_____

_____

_____

_____

_____

_____

_____

_____

_____

_____

_____

_____

_____

_____

_____

_____

_____

_____

Chapter 9: The Business Plan—an Overview

The Name Game

How you present yourself and your business is important to potential investors, bankers, and customers. The name that you select should help sell your product. A good business name should be memorable and should communicate what the business is all about. If the quality of your business is revealed in the name, you will advertise your product every time people see the name of your business.

This activity presents business descriptions and corresponding business names. Evaluate each example and determine if the name is memorable and communicates the nature of the business. If not, create a new name for the company. If the name is a good one for the business being described, explain why you think the name does not need to be changed. Two examples are given to help you get started.

Business Description	Business Name	Revised Name/ Explanation
Example: Dry cleaning service for executives	Fifth Avenue Cleaners	The Golden Hanger or Executive Cleaners
Example: Bookstore with an attached cafe	Nickleby's Bookstore/ Cafe	Name is memorable (invokes a Dickens novel) and communicates the type of business.
1. Coffee house specializing in cheesecakes	The Coffee Table	_____ _____ _____ _____ _____
2. Frame shop	The Frame Station	_____ _____ _____ _____ _____

Chapter 9: The Business Plan—an Overview

Variations on a Theme

There are many shapes and sizes of business plans. As you gather information on your own entrepreneurial venture, the format you will want to use will probably suggest itself to you. In the meantime, this activity will present you with two more options. Study these business plan outlines. Then compare and contrast them by answering the questions on the next two pages.

Variation A

I. Description and analysis of proposed business
  A. Type of business
  B. Business philosophy
  C. Description of good/service
  D. Self-analysis
    1. Education and training
    2. Strengths and weaknesses
    3. Plan for personal development
  E. Trade area analysis
    1. Geographic, demographic, and economic data
    2. Competition
  F. Market segment analysis
    1. Target market
    2. Customer buying behavior
  G. Analysis of potential location
II. Organization and marketing plan
  A. Proposed organization
    1. Type of ownership
    2. Steps in establishing business
    3. Personnel needs
  B. Proposed good/service
    1. Manufacturing plans, inventory policies
    2. Suppliers
  C. Proposed marketing plan
    1. Pricing policies
    2. Promotional activities
III. Financial plan
  A. Sources of capital
    1. Personal sources
    2. External sources
  B. Projected income and expenses
    1. Personal financial statement
    2. Personal balance sheet
    3. Income statement(s)
    4. Projected start-up costs
    5. Projected personal needs
    6. Projected business income
    7. Projected business expenses
    8. Projected cash flow

Variation B

I. Executive summary
II. Management and organization
  A. Management team
  B. Compensation
  C. Advisory council
  D. Organization chart
III. Service plan
  A. Purpose
  B. Unique features
  C. Trademarks and copyrights
  D. Product liability
  E. Related services and spin-offs
  F. Production
  G. Environmental factors
IV. Marketing plan
  A. Industry profile
  B. Competition profile
  C. Customer profile
  D. Target market profile
  E. Advertising and promotion
  F. Trade shows
  G. Pricing profile
  H. Future markets
V. Financial plan
  A. Assumptions
  B. Cash flows
  C. Income statements
  D. Balance sheets
VI. Operations
  A. Administrative policies
  B. Administrative controls
  C. Risk analysis
VII. Growth plan
  A. New services
  B. Capital requirements
  C. Personnel requirements
  D. Exit strategy
VIII. Appendix
  A. Resumes
  B. Sample contracts and agreements
  C. Sample advertisements

Name _____ Date _____

1. Do an outline of the business plan structure described in Chapter 9 of your text. Try to duplicate the level of detail shown in the outlines on the previous page.

_____   _____

_____   _____

_____   _____

_____   _____

_____   _____

_____   _____

_____   _____

2. How is the first outline (Variation A) different from the business plan structure presented in your text?

_____

_____

_____

_____

_____

_____

3. How is the second outline (Variation B) different from the business plan structure presented in your text?

_____

_____

_____

_____

_____

_____

4. What elements (if any) do all three outlines share? (In other words, how are they similar?)

_____

_____

_____

_____

_____

_____

5. Can you think of any instances in which one business plan format might be better than the other? Explain.

_____

_____

_____

_____

_____

_____

6. List below any entries from the outlines that you do not recognize or understand. Use your text's glossary and index and any available class-room references to try to develop simple definitions for these terms.

_____   _____

_____   _____

_____   _____

_____   _____

_____   _____

_____   _____

Chapter 10: Market Analysis

Name That Target Market

The first step in doing a market analysis is identification of your market—the group of people or companies who have a demand for your product and are willing and able to buy it. In order to make the most effective and efficient appeal to potential customers, you should divide the total market into smaller segments. You can then appeal to the special interests or needs of one of those segments—your target market.

Market analysts have coined terms to refer to specific market segments. Some of these are listed below and on the next page. For each group listed, identify three specialized goods or services that would have a special appeal and explain why.

Target Group	Description
1. Dinks	Double income, no kids

a. _____

_____

b. _____

_____

c. _____

_____

2. Woofs	Well-off, over fifty

a. _____

_____

b. _____

_____

c. _____

_____

3. Skippies	School kids with income and purchasing power

a. _____

_____

Target Group   **Description**

b. _____

_____

_____

c. _____

_____

_____

4. Swaks   Single woman and kids

a. _____

_____

_____

b. _____

_____

_____

c. _____

_____

_____

5. Swank   Single woman and no kids

a. _____

_____

_____

b. _____

_____

_____

c. _____

_____

_____

Chapter 10: Market Analysis

Say Cheese!

Read the following article. Then analyze the market segments based on the questions that follow.

The Hottest Thing Since the Flashbulb

Slow to develop, disposables have become a $200 million market

The guests at Diane and L. J. Palazesi's wedding in Boston earlier this year found a surprise on each table: a disposable camera. Afraid the professional photographer would miss those spontaneous moments that define a wedding, the bride and groom bought a dozen of the $11 cameras and invited guests to take candid snaps. Several hours and hundreds of flashes later, guests simply dumped the cameras in a bag to be shipped off to the developer. "We got a lot of really fun pictures," says Diane. "It was a great idea."

Fun. Cheap. Easy to use. That potent combination has turned the disposable camera—basically a roll of film with a cheap plastic case and lens—into the hottest thing in photography. Sales in the U.S. zoomed 50% last year, with no sign of leveling off... Projected sales for 1992 are 22 million units in the U.S., or about $200 million at retail. "I could see sales tripling or even quadrupling within three years," says Joel B. Streeter, camera buyer at Kmart Corp., which is so enthusiastic that it has granted disposables coveted space at its checkout counters. To make sure enthusiasm doesn't wane, Eastman Kodak Co., with about 65% of the market for disposables, and Fuji Photo Film USA Inc., with about 25%, are rolling out niche products for everything from underwater photography to close-ups of baby.

It's a pleasant surprise for the amateur film business in the U.S., where retail sales have stayed flat since 1989 at 750 million rolls, or about $2.1 billion a year. "It's been a real shot in the arm," says Rod H. King, senior marketing manager at Fuji Photo.

When Fuji pioneered disposable cameras in Japan in 1986, few in the film business expected them to click. After all, most people already had cameras. And disposables were slow to catch on in the U.S., where they were introduced by Kodak in late 1987.

But as the public grew more familiar with the product, the disposable started to sell itself by filling needs that regular cameras can't. One giant need: being there when your fancy Minolta or Canon isn't.

Peter M. Palermo, general manager of Kodak's consumer imaging division, figures about half of the purchases are made by people who left their regular cameras at home. Buying a new camera would be extravagant; an $8 to $12 disposable is cheap by comparison, even with the added cost of processing. "Don't think of it as a camera, think of it as convenient film," says John J. Ruf, a partner at New England Consulting Group in Westport, Conn.

Film marketers also figure that at least half the photos taken with disposables wouldn't have been shot otherwise, as buyers keep finding new uses for the devices. Wedding snaps like the Palazesis' are a hot growth area. Truck drivers now use disposables to record accident scenes. The cameras also appeal to teens and senior citizens who find regular cameras either daunting to use or too pricey to buy. As for quality, disposables are still no match for expensive 35 mm cameras. But since they use 35 mm film, they produce better-quality photos than those old Instamatics...

Now, Kodak and Fuji are mixing different film speeds, lenses, and accessories to tailor disposables to almost any need. Standing on the edge of the Grand Canyon? Disposables can take panoramic, wide-angle shots. Snorkeling? Focus on that flounder with an underwater disposable. Sports fans are another target: Kodak now markets a telephoto version with ultrafast 1600 ASA film for the stadium set. The company sold 4,000 of these through a special vendor at last year's Super Bowl. Kodak planners are looking at a model equipped with a short focal-length lens and fast film requiring less light to capture an image. They figure parents would like this disposable to take snapshots of their babies without the disturbing flash.

There's room for even more market segmentation. Just look at camera-happy Japan, where disposables now capture more than 10% of the film market, vs. 3% in the U.S. In one Japanese catalog aimed at young women, Kodak sells a package of five pastel-colored cameras for $70, including a version with a fish-eye lens and another with a foggy lens to create a rosy, romantic glow. For the film industry, disposables are about the only product around that's even remotely rosy.

By Mark Maremont in Boston,
with Robert Neff in Tokyo.

Reprinted from September 7, 1992 issue of *Business Week* by special permission, copyright © 1992 by McGraw-Hill, Inc.

1. What is the market for the disposable camera?

_____

_____

_____

_____

_____

_____

2. Identify the market segments referred to in the article.

_____

_____

_____

_____

_____

_____

_____

_____

_____

_____

_____

_____

_____

_____

_____

_____

3. Identify three additional market segments for the camera. Give the characteristics of each segment, and describe how you would position the camera to reach each of these new target markets.

_____

_____

_____

_____

_____

_____

_____

_____

_____

_____

_____

_____

_____

_____

_____

_____

_____

_____

_____

_____

_____

_____

_____

3. How will you determine your sales potential?

_____

_____

_____

_____

_____

_____

_____

4. Who is your competition?

_____

_____

_____

_____

_____

_____

_____

5. How will you conduct market research?

_____

_____

_____

_____

_____

_____

_____

_____

Chapter 11: The Marketing Mix

Denim for All

Developing a creative, well thought-out marketing plan is critical to the success of any business. It is particularly critical, however, to a small business serving the needs of a specific target market.

In the Decisions case study for this chapter, you read about an entrepreneur who is starting a denim wear shop for males and females, 16–24 years old. Below you will find an expanded review of the information about this proposed business. By answering the questions on the next several pages, you will be developing a preliminary marketing plan.

Each section of this activity will address one of the four P's of the marketing mix. Exploring these strategies is very important not only to the success of this business but also your own. The questions you ask and ideas you propose may prove to be important as you develop the marketing plan for your own business.

Business Description

Denim for All will be a denim wear shop for males and females, 16–24 years old, living within your county. Its product mix will consist of jeans and other casual clothes in denim—also, bib overalls and denim jackets for young children. The business might even expand to add tennis shoes and sweat suits.

The location of the business will be a leased space in a building a few miles outside of town. There aren't any other retailers there, and there's not much traffic, but there is plenty of parking, and the rent is low. The hours of operation will be 10 A.M.–5 P.M.

Prices will be set just above cost. The rationale is that once customers find out what bargains are being offered, they'll keep coming back for more.

Promotion will be used to get customers to drive the distance out to the store. Good rates are available for early morning TV spots (5–7 A.M.). Also, there will be billboards on the road to the store. No salespeople will be hired because customers who come to the store will know exactly what they want. This will also help keep prices down.

A. Product Decisions

As you develop the product strategy for this start-up business, answer the following questions. *Hint:* Keep the target market in mind as you decide on your answers.

1. Who is the target market for Denim for All? Is the target group too broad or too narrow? Explain.

_____

_____

_____

Entrepreneurship and Small Business Management **67**

_____

_____

_____

_____

_____

_____

2. What products should Denim for All sell? (Are there products proposed that should be eliminated? Are there additional products that could enhance the product mix? Explain.)

_____

_____

_____

_____

_____

_____

_____

3. How will the products offered by Denim for All be different from or better than the products offered by the competition?

_____

_____

_____

_____

_____

_____

_____

4. How would you position the store's products?

_____

_____

_____

_____

_____

_____

B. Pricing Decisions

    As you develop the pricing strategy for this start-up business, keep in mind your pricing goals. How can pricing help you achieve your business objectives? Would lower prices help you beat the competition and obtain market share? Would higher prices give you a better return on your investment?

1. What is the pricing strategy that the owner of Denim for All is proposing?

_____

_____

_____

_____

_____

_____

2. Based on the strategy proposed, has the owner considered all of the factors in determining prices? Explain.

_____

_____

_____

_____

_____

_____

_____

         Entrepreneurship and Small Business Management   **69**

3. What type of pricing strategy would you propose? Explain the
reasons for your choice.

_____

_____

_____

_____

_____

_____

4. What motivates the customers who will buy from this store? Are
they primarily price sensitive or status conscious? Explain.

_____

_____

_____

_____

_____

_____

5. Which would you use—psychological pricing or prestige pricing?
Explain the importance of this technique in motivating your
target market.

_____

_____

_____

_____

_____

_____

_____

C. Place Decisions

Place strategy involves how you will deliver your goods and services to your customers. Where will they buy? When will they buy? Will your product actually be available and ready for sale?

1. Is the location described appropriate for the business's target market(s)? Why or why not? If not, what would you propose as an alternate location?

_____

_____

_____

_____

_____

2. What would you propose for the physical layout of the business? Provide a brief description and explain how the layout will encourage sales. Then create a rough sketch in the space at the bottom of the page.

_____

_____

_____

_____

_____

Entrepreneurship and Small Business Management

3. From which channel members will the business obtain its products?

_____

_____

_____

_____

_____

4. Do the hours of operation match the times that the target market prefers to do business? Explain.

_____

_____

_____

_____

_____

_____

_____

_____

5. What would you propose for the business's hours of operation? Explain how these hours would address the concerns of the target market.

_____

_____

_____

_____

_____

_____

_____

D. Promotion Decisions

The promotional strategy should tell customers about your product or business's benefits and availability.

1. What type of advertising media has the owner proposed to use? Will these be effective? Explain why or why not.

_____

_____

_____

_____

_____

_____

_____

2. What kind of advertising media would you propose? Why?

_____

_____

_____

_____

_____

_____

_____

3. What would you suggest for an advertising message or theme? Elaborate.

_____

_____

_____

_____

_____

_____

Entrepreneurship and Small Business Management

4. What sales promotion devices and activities would be appropriate for
this business? Explain.

_____

_____

_____

_____

_____

_____

_____

_____

_____

_____

5. Should the business incorporate personal selling? Why or why not?

_____

_____

_____

_____

_____

_____

_____

_____

_____

_____

Chapter 12: Legal Requirements

Gotcha!

Mrs. Hazelton had dreamed for years of opening a crafts boutique that would sell products made by local artists. She even had a name—Earth Designs—and knew the shop would concentrate on products made from natural materials. Mrs. Hazelton had even spoken to a few artists who agreed to let her sell their work. Finally, she had enough commitments to open her business.

She decided that she would start the business in her garage and would open three days a week—Friday, Saturday, and Sunday. She lived in a nice residential neighborhood, got along well with her neighbors, and saw this as an inexpensive way to begin.

She advertised the opening of her shop and on her first weekend was very successful. She was, therefore, shocked when the following week she received a letter informing her that she was violating a number of local laws regarding business operation. In the letter she was told to shut her boutique immediately.

1. Having read Chapter 12, how could you have helped Mrs. Hazelton in starting her business? What local laws might she have violated?

_____

_____

_____

_____

_____

_____

_____

2. Assume Mrs. Hazelton did nothing else in starting up her business except what was described above. Name one other legal pitfall she might have encountered.

_____

_____

_____

_____

_____

_____

Entrepreneurship and Small Business Management

Chapter 12: Legal Requirements

The Creation of a Partnership

John and Cecil have decided to start an after-school business. Their school has numerous activities every afternoon in which many parents, teachers, and students are involved. John and Cecil noticed that these people often walk to a nearby grocery store to buy snacks and drinks while they are waiting.

The boys have determined a need and have designed a way to meet it. They want to open a stand that will offer hot food and snacks right on the school grounds. To do so, they will enter into a contract with the school. The contract will include a provision that 20 percent of the stand's profits will be placed in a fund to provide new library books. The remaining profits will be split between the two owner-operators.

Help John and Cecil begin their new business by answering the questions below. Imagine that it's you and a friend starting this business. How would you find out what legal requirements you must meet? *Hint:* Your county or state health departments can answer questions about the legal requirements for food service businesses.

1. What licenses or permits might John and Cecil need?

_____

_____

_____

_____

_____

_____

2. What other legal requirements will they need to meet in order to operate their food stand?

_____

_____

_____

_____

_____

_____

3. Do a first draft of a contract between John and Cecil and the school.
   Note: Do not be concerned with John and Cecil's capacity.

_____

_____

_____

_____

_____

_____

_____

_____

_____

_____

_____

_____

_____

_____

_____

_____

_____

_____

_____

_____

_____

_____

Entrepreneurship and Small Business Management

4. Do a first draft of a contract between John and Cecil. *Note:* Do not be
concerned with their capacity.

_____

_____

_____

_____

_____

_____

_____

_____

_____

_____

_____

_____

_____

_____

_____

_____

_____

_____

_____

_____

_____

Chapter 12: Legal Requirements

What Came First—Max or the Chicken?

Max Everneedy, owner of Max's Meats, feels that he needs to run a new radio ad to help stimulate sagging sales in his poultry and fish business. This new ad will focus on chicken. He hopes it will bring more people into his store and generate new business. Here is the copy for the new radio ad.

"Max's Meats is having a sale on chickens at our lowest prices ever! These are the plumpest, leanest, healthiest chickens available anywhere. Eating these chickens is guaranteed to lower your cholesterol level and strengthen your heart. Recent reports confirm that eating chicken adds years to your life by reducing the overall fat in your system.

"At Max's Meats you can now purchase these marvels of culinary delight at unbelievable prices. You will never find a better deal than this. Hurry over to Max's, the place where stingy shoppers shop."

Max has no idea where his chickens come from, nor does he know their fat content or anything else about them. While his chicken prices are in fact the lowest in town, his "sale" price is 25 cents higher than his regular price.

Max does know, however, that he will shortly be facing a supply crunch as a result of losses incurred by farmers during a major winter storm. He rationalizes that he can offer turkey or fish at slightly reduced prices if he runs out. He also figures that after running the ad for a few days he can raise his prices to match his competitors' on whatever stock he has left. After all, the ad doesn't specify how long the prices are good. Max figures he'll just play it by ear and make up his own.

1. How do this ad and Max's attitude conflict with truth-in-advertising guidelines?

_____

_____

_____

_____

_____

_____

_____

_____

_____

_____

2. If you were to rewrite the ad, what would it say?

_____

_____

_____

_____

_____

_____

_____

_____

_____

_____

_____

_____

_____

_____

_____

_____

_____

_____

_____

_____

_____

_____

Chapter 13: Equipment, Supplies, and Inventory

Let Your Fingers Do the Walking

The Yellow Pages is a valuable source of information for would-be entrepreneurs doing their start-up planning. It is especially valuable when a new owner is contemplating equipment, supply, and inventory decisions.

Assume you want to open a catering business operating out of a small storefront. You know that you will have to outfit a kitchen for the business (the property has no existing facilities). To get some ideas for how to go about doing this, you look in the phone book under Restaurant Suppliers and find the page shown below. Study it carefully, and then answer the questions on the following two pages.

© Pacific Bell Directory 1992 SD

Name _____ Date _____

1. According to the ads shown, what other options do you have besides buying brand-new equipment?

_____

_____

_____

_____

_____

2. Besides selling equipment, what other services do the listed suppliers commonly provide?

_____

_____

_____

_____

_____

3. What are some of the more unusual services that listed suppliers provide?

_____

_____

_____

_____

4. What different types of equipment do the various suppliers sell?

_____

_____

_____

_____

_____

5. Judging from the ads, with what sorts of customers are the listed suppliers accustomed to dealing?

_____

_____

_____

_____

_____

6. What sorts of additional information do listed suppliers include in their ads either to inspire confidence in the reader or to distinguish themselves from their competitors?

_____

_____

_____

_____

_____

_____

_____

_____

7. What payment options do the listed suppliers give their customers?

_____

_____

_____

_____

_____

_____

_____

_____

Chapter 13: Equipment, Supplies, and Inventory

Smart Buys

Read the article that appears on the next three pages, and answer the questions that follow.

A Key for a Macy Comeback

A new system of allocating goods is at the heart of a 5-year plan.

By Stephanie Strom

When R.H. Macy & Company presents its five-year business plan to its creditors on Thursday, much of it will be devoted to an unusual new system of allocating merchandise. Bland as that might sound, the company thinks it will be the cornerstone of its effort to leave bankruptcy behind and emerge as a profitable retailer.

The system, begun successfully in Macy's men's division a year ago and since rolled out in the rest of the company, introduces a new traffic cop, known as a planner, between the merchandise buyer and the store itself. Tracking sales data compiled each time a clerk rings up a sale in a Macy's store, the planner spots selling patterns store by store and advises the buyer on what to buy and what not to buy for each of the 112 stores. The planner also advises each store on what and how much to stock.

In the past, Macy's allocation of merchandise was much more hit and miss—the company had little or no idea what was selling in stores and what wasn't until weeks later and so could not respond smartly.

Just how well the new system works became clear to Macy in an example like this: The company recently had an East Coast sale on men's shirts that was identical to one a year earlier. Yet Macy's sold 30 percent more shirts. The reason: A planner studied the computer numbers on last year's sale and found that many stores had sold out of the shirts quickly. He told the buyer, who then ordered more shirts to meet the demand.

Another example is sales of Hanes hosiery. Thanks to a planner responding to sales data generated by the computer, Macy has increased its business 15 percent on 25 percent less inventory. And because of a direct new computer link between Macy's and Hanes, orders that used to take up to seven weeks to complete are now filled in nine days.

The new system is crucial for Macy because as margins shrink under growing competition, the emphasis in retailing is increasingly on turnover. And shoppers will more likely find what they want, in the size and color. But the item will be less likely to be marked down, because Macy's can better anticipate demand.

"This is a jugular issue, a major change from the way we conducted our business," said Mark S. Handler, co-chairman of Macy. "How you assort and distribute a product is as important as what you buy."

That is a phenomenal change of heart for a merchant who cut his teeth in Macy's training program, which taught young executives the more-is-always-better-than-less theory of inventory management. Such a system guaranteed that the stores always had a lot of merchandise, but also guaranteed that they carried not only best-sellers but also many goods they couldn't give away.

Now, with the zeal of the newly converted, Mr. Handler and Lawrence Anderson are preaching that less is sometimes more. "We're buying less but more appropriately and therefore selling more," said Mr. Anderson, group vice president of men's planning and distribution. "It's a significant change in our culture."

Stocking the colors and sizes its customers want increases Macy's chances of selling more and making those sales more profitable. A study of Macy's customers after the company filed for bankruptcy indicated that they were frequently disappointed because the Macy's store in their neighborhood was out of stock in what they wanted. Kurt Salmon Associates, the consulting and research firm that conducted the study, estimated that Macy could increase its sales by 17 percent simply by carrying the right stock.

Consultants and analysts wonder whether Macy can really institute such a change. The company did not disclose details of how its new system works until it briefed. *The New York Times* 10 days ago, and therefore few people have enough information to assess it. But getting employees to accept new computers and a new way of doing business will take years, they say, and Macy doesn't have years to reverse losses like the $1.25 billion loss it reported on Friday for its fiscal year, which ended Aug. 1.

"It's going to take time because Macy's is an institution, but I think there is at least the direction that they didn't have before," said Walter F. Loeb, president of Loeb Associates Inc., a retail consulting firm.

With the installation of computerized inventory management and accounting systems and the new buying system, Macy has estimated that its cash flow will exceed $800 million by 1998. Without any of the changes, cash flow—or earnings before interest, taxes, depreciation and amortization—would be $210 million.

Mr. Anderson says the improvement in turnover they have seen will make believers out of the worst skeptics. "We're seeing success, and it has happened a lot sooner than we expected," Mr. Anderson said.

In its Southern stores, where Macy first began the process, the company has increased revenues and profits, said Myron (Mike) E. Ullman 3d, Macy's co-chairman. The system now operates across the nation, which is broken into East and West divisions. "While it's premature to say we've seen overwhelming improvement across both divisions, we have seen marked improvement in the area we've had it longest," he said.

Mr. Ullman said the five-year business plan assumes that the company will experience no real growth during that period, which means incredible pressure to reduce expenses and raise productivity. "The old system worked great when we were growing 8 percent a year," he said.

When the company stopped growing, however, its bloated management and excessive inventory became apparent. In the quarter following its bankruptcy filing last Jan. 27, Macy wrote off more than $300 million in worthless inventory.

Macy's new system does add a layer of managers—a few more than 100 planners, all former buyers. On the other hand, Macy's has cut the number of buyers to 180 from 425. The remaining positions were eliminated, reducing costs. Because compensation for each buyer, planner and store manager now depends to some extent on the performance of the troika as a whole, it is intended to increase cooperation among the three.

Under the old system, stores called the buyers directly to ask for merchandise. The buyer for junior apparel, for example, could get calls from more than 50 stores in his division, on top of his duties planning advertising and promotions, calling on suppliers, ordering, allocating merchandise to the stores and worrying about whether he was making his gross margin targets. Buyers were infamous for not returning calls until days after they were made, squandering the opportunity to sell more merchandise.

"When I was a buyer, I dreaded talking to the stores because when they called me, it was usually to complain," said Max Weisenfeld, the planner for men's dress shirts in Macy's eastern division.

But now the stores rely on the planner to tell the buyer what they need. For example, thanks to a computer system that tells planner, buyer and store manager precisely what's selling where, Pattie McCluskey, the planner responsible for certain men's apparel, knows that orange Polo shirts don't sell in Smith Haven, L.I. (The reason is that a substantial number of the store's customers work for the local public-works department and wear orange uniforms five days a week. They prefer other colors during their leisure time. So Macy's has started stocking—and selling—more shirts in navy, red and forest green.)

"We can now treat every store like it is the only store in the world," Mr. Weisenfeld said. Some stores are known as fat stores because more of their customers buy larger sizes; others are "skinny" stores. Others sell a disproportionate amount of tennis togs, and some sell more black.

With people like Ms. McCluskey and Mr. Weisenfeld serving as traffic cops and the computer providing the information needed to direct the traffic, Neal Goldberg, who manages the Macy's store in Bridgewater, N.J., no longer has to write long memos arguing that knit shirts outsell woven shirts among the country-club set that makes up his customers. "I now have time to be out on the floor selling goods and getting a feel for my business," Mr. Goldberg said, "instead of spending time on the telephone in the office trying to first reach a buyer and then convince him that I need more goods."

1. Describe the key change that Macy's is making when ordering stock.

_____

_____

_____

_____

_____

_____

_____

_____

_____

_____

_____

_____

_____

_____

_____

_____

_____

_____

_____

2. Explain the statement in the article that "less is sometimes more."

_____

_____

_____

_____

_____

_____

_____

_____

_____

_____

_____

_____

_____

3. Why is it so important that a business be accurate when purchasing inventory?

_____

_____

_____

_____

_____

_____

_____

_____

Entrepreneurship and Small Business Management

_____

_____

_____

_____

4. What is the role and importance of the planner in this situation?

_____

_____

_____

_____

_____

_____

_____

_____

_____

_____

_____

_____

_____

_____

_____

_____

_____

_____

5. Diagram the flow of information both before and after planners were added to Macy's inventory control system.

Before:

After:

Chapter 14: Site Selection

Kiosk—a "Clean" Look

Below is a case study about a student who wants to start a very service-oriented dry cleaning business. As you read it, think of yourself as someone who is going to start a similar business in a different area. What would you want to find out about the site? What would make such a business successful? How would you find out? After you read the case study, answer the questions that follow.

One student entrepreneur was contemplating the start-up of a dry cleaning business—with a difference. This dry cleaner would be located in a kiosk in a San Francisco subway station. Subway commuters would be able to drop off their dry cleaning in the morning as they went to work and pick it up in the late afternoon on their way home.

To learn about the best place to locate his kiosk, the student studied the site chosen by his only competitor. During the morning and evening rush hours, he sat out of the way and counted the number of people who either dropped off or picked up dry cleaning on their way to and from trains. In this way he found out more about the demand for the service. He also gained information about how accessible and desirable the particular site was.

1. You are planning to travel to the existing kiosk site to evaluate it for yourself. What would you try to find out through your observations? Make a list of questions that would help you determine why the existing business is successful in its present location.

_____

_____

_____

_____

_____

_____

_____

_____

_____

_____

_____

2. How would you transfer the information from San Francisco to a
location in your own community? What would you need to do?

_____

_____

_____

_____

_____

_____

_____

_____

_____

3. If you had the opportunity to interview the owner of the original dry
cleaning kiosk, what questions would you want to ask? (List at least four.)

_____

_____

_____

_____

_____

_____

_____

_____

_____

_____

Chapter 14: Site Selection

Cheese Danish To Go

You want to start a small bakery to service small restaurants and cafes with breads, pastries, and other limited items. However, you would also like to have some foot traffic. Before you choose your site, ask (and answer) the following important questions.

1. What are the important site considerations for this type of business?

_____

_____

_____

_____

_____

_____

_____

_____

_____

_____

_____

_____

_____

_____

_____

_____

_____

_____

_____

_____

_____

2. What would you need to do first? How would you begin your search?

_____

_____

_____

_____

_____

_____

_____

_____

3. What steps would you take to determine your probability for success in
a particular location?

_____

_____

_____

_____

_____

_____

_____

_____

_____

_____

Chapter 14: Site Selection

Crazy Locations

Some businesses are just so offbeat that they invite their creators to defy conventional thinking about a host of considerations—including site selection. Below is a list of such businesses. Your task is to find an equally offbeat location for each. (You may even see how some could be incorporated into existing businesses.)

So, have some fun, and allow your imagination to run wild. Remember, however, that even though the location you recommend might be a bit crazy, you still need to show a connection between it and the needs of the business.

1. **Laid-Back Life-style Gifts.** This company has a line of products including thongs with cleats on the bottom and other humorous gear for "laid-back" golfers, fishers, and hunters. Almost all of the company's merchandise is either funny or fun—and it is all unique.

_____

_____

_____

_____

2. **Used Rubber, USA.** This store sells fashion accessories made from old tires and inner tubes.

_____

_____

_____

_____

3. **Bento Express.** This Japanese restaurant offers teriyaki-laced Spam "sushi" at lunch. It's a big seller.

_____

_____

_____

_____

4. **Cow Pie Clocks.** A brother-and-sister team make clocks from cow pies they find in local pastures.

_____

_____

_____

_____

_____

5. **Black Jewel Popcorn.** This company sells black food, deemed the latest in culinary delights—black popcorn, black rice, black olives, black mushrooms, black pasta, black beans.

_____

_____

_____

_____

_____

6. **Designer Bands.** This business sells surgical bandages overlaid with different colors of laces, rhinestones, and pearls—for about $2.50 each.

_____

_____

_____

_____

_____

7. **The Ravioli Store.** This take-out business sells 11 types of ravioli at $3.50–$9.00 a pound. Flavors include jalapeno, chocolate, and lobster.

_____

_____

_____

_____

_____

Chapter 15: Physical Layout

Have I Got a Plan for You!

You have been in many types of business establishments—grocery stores, quick marts, hair stylists, video stores, and many others. In each case, you probably made some judgments about the business. In all likelihood, however, you sensed things rather than consciously noted them. You knew, for example, whether the business was easy to get around in. You knew whether you found it interesting. You knew whether you felt welcome.

Now that you have read Chapter 15, you know the source of many of these perceptions. You know that layout is essential to the development of a successful business.

Think of a business that you have been in that might be enhanced by improving its layout plan. Then, try to redesign that plan, using the six objectives listed in the chapter and the questions given with them below. *Note:* After you have completed this exercise, you may want to share your plan with the business owner or manager.

1. **Define the objectives of the facility.** What is the space used for— sales, storage, production? Be as specific as possible.

   _____

   _____

   _____

   _____

   _____

   _____

   _____

   _____

   _____

   _____

   _____

   _____

   _____

2. **Identify the primary and supporting activities take place in the facility.** List as many as you can for both staff and customers.

_____   _____

_____   _____

_____   _____

_____   _____

_____   _____

3. **Determine the interrelationships among all the activities.** How are the activities above related to each other? How does one activity affect another?

_____

_____

_____

_____

_____

_____

4. **Determine the space requirements for all activities.** Do you think your chosen business has enough space—or the right kind of space—for the activities listed above? If so, estimate how much has been given over to each activity. If not, estimate how much space you think should be given over to each. What do you think the space requirements should be for all activities mentioned?

_____

_____

_____

_____

_____

_____

_____

5. Design an alternative layout for the facility. You may use the space below or develop a layout on additional paper.

6. Evaluate the layout. Explain how your new layout is an improvement over the existing one.

_____

_____

_____

_____

_____

_____

_____

Chapter 15: Physical Layout

Keep It Moving!

The layout of a retail business has a critical impact on sales and, therefore, profits. As you may recall from Chapter 15, the most important design consideration is the flow of customers through the operation.

On the next page is the layout for an actual public market called The North Market. It currently consists of 28 family-owned businesses. These businesses are engaged primarily in the sale of unprepared foods, such as meat, poultry, produce, and dairy products. The market facility is currently housed in a World War II surplus Quonset hut. Within this facility, there is no room for expansion of selling space or any addition of businesses.

As you review the layout, pay attention to the variety and types of merchants, perceived clientele, product coordination, aisle exposure, and traffic flow. After you review the market's layout and the types of businesses housed there, answer the questions that begin on this page and continue on page 102.

1. How would you describe the layout of merchants within the North Market? Explain.

_____

_____

_____

_____

_____

_____

_____

_____

_____

_____

_____

_____

_____

_____

_____

Farmer's Market

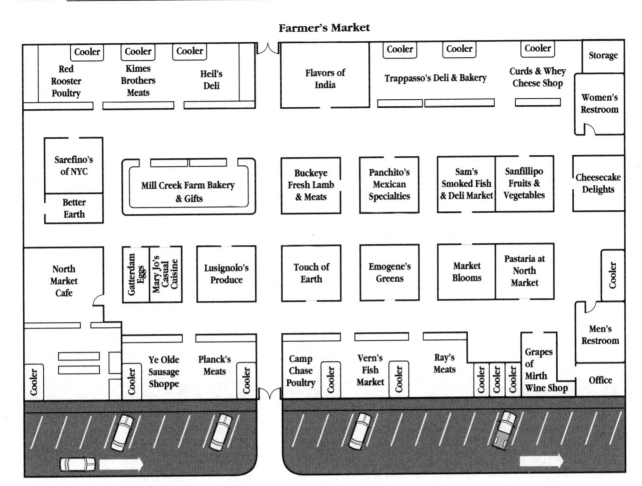

2. Do you think this layout is effective for this type of market facility? Why or why not?

_____

_____

_____

_____

_____

_____

_____

3. Are there barriers to customer movement in the current market? Explain.

_____

_____

_____

_____

_____

_____

4. Given this type of selling environment, discuss the advantages and disadvantages of product coordination (placing the same type of merchants in the same section of the market).

_____

_____

_____

_____

_____

_____

_____

Chapter 16: Protecting Your Business

Is It Worth the Risk?

One of the many issues you will face as an entrepreneur is how to protect your business from various kinds of risk. Chapter 16 discusses four separate strategies for dealing with risk—avoidance, reduction, transfer, and retention.

Each of the examples below falls into one of these categories. Assume that you are the entrepreneur in each instance, and decide which form of risk management is being used. Write your answers in the appropriate blanks.

1. _____ You decide to purchase business interruption insurance.

2. _____ You put flood lamps at each exterior corner of the store.

3. _____ You hire someone to scrape the parking lot and shovel the entryway when there is a snowfall.

4. _____ You teach your stockroom employees how to lift heavy boxes so as to avoid back injuries.

5. _____ You choose not to carry a line of products that appears to be especially easy to shoplift.

6. _____ You have a qualified person check the fire extinguishers in your place of business each month.

7. _____ You purchase fire insurance.

8. _____ You pay workers compensation each month.

9. _____ You save a percentage of profits each month to guard against short-term economic downturns.

10. _____ You install electronic sensors to discourage shoplifting.

11. _____ You have a silent alarm system installed that signals the nearest police station.

12. _____ You instruct employees in the use of potentially dangerous equipment.

13. _____ You move your store from an isolated corner to a busy mall.

14. _____ You hold employee meetings to discuss ways of reducing accidents.

15. _____ In response to what you believe to be exorbitantly high premiums, you decide to drop your property insurance and self-insure instead.

16. _____ You bond your employees who handle cash.

Entrepreneurship and Small Business Management   **103**

17. _____ You educate your employees in the storage and handling of hazardous substances they must use on the job.

18. _____ When it rains, you place nonskid floor mats in the entryways of your business.

19. _____ You contract with a local security firm to patrol your business premises at night.

20. _____ You establish bonding insurance for your employees through your business.

21. _____ When it rains, you place rubber mats in the entryways of your business.

22. _____ You provide your employees with first aid and CPR training.

23. _____ You add uninsured and underinsured motorists coverage to the policy you already have for your business's delivery vans.

24. _____ Because you can't afford health insurance for yourself or your family, you make regular deposits to a bank account you maintain for coping with health care emergencies.

25. _____ You make regular payments to your state's workers compensation plan.

26. _____ You elect not to make COD deliveries and advertise this fact by placing "Driver carries no cash" stickers on the windows of your delivery vans.

27. _____ You install an electronic credit authorizer by your cash register.

28. _____ You place signs at key points around the sales floor and near exits, indicating that shoplifters will be prosecuted to the full limits of the law.

29. _____ You provide your employees with safety gear and see that it is used routinely and properly.

Chapter 16: Protecting Your Business

To Take a Risk—or Not

Lisa and Phil have decided to expand their catering business to accommodate larger orders and to offer in-home preparation. However, this expansion will mean hiring additional help and dealing with increased business risks. The services the catering business will offer include planning and pre-event preparation, transportation of equipment and personnel to events, and on-site preparation of food. Events will include business functions and private parties.

Until now Lisa and Phil have not had to be too concerned with risks. They were the only ones involved in the business, and most of their clients were friends. But now they have to consider risk management. Help them by providing answers to the questions below. Rely on information presented in the chapter and your own entrepreneurial instincts.

1. What are the risks you can identify for Lisa and Phil? Try to think of at least ten.

   a. _____

   _____

   b. _____

   _____

   c. _____

   _____

   d. _____

   _____

   e. _____

   _____

   f. _____

   _____

   g. _____

   _____

   h. _____

   _____

   i. _____

   _____

   j. _____

   _____

   _____

   _____

2. What advice would you give Lisa and Phil about developing a risk management plan? (*Note:* The plan should cover all of the risks you identified on the preceding page and provide recommendations for dealing with them.)

_____

_____

_____

_____

_____

_____

_____

_____

_____

_____

_____

_____

_____

_____

_____

_____

_____

_____

_____

_____

Chapter 17: Operations and Staffing

Watch Out! Here Comes the EEOC!

In Chapter 17, you learned about the importance of recruiting and selecting employees as you begin to build your business. In previous chapters (12 and 16), you also learned about what you can and cannot legally ask in an interview.

The following dialogue is between a small business owner and an individual who is interviewing for a job. (The business owner is referred to as *OWN*, the interviewee as *INT*.) Study the interview carefully, looking for examples of illegal questions or those that you feel are simply improper. Also, think about what would be appropriate responses under the circumstances depicted. Use your conclusions to answer the questions that appear on pages 109 and 110.

OWN:　Good morning, Mrs. Ward. It is *Mrs.* Ward, isn't it? In this day of women's lib you can never tell, you know. My name is Mr. Winthrop. Have a seat.

INT:　Thank you, Mr. Winthrop.

OWN:　You're a very attractive woman. How old are you?

INT:　I happen to be 35.

OWN:　Hmmmmmm. I understand that you're here to interview for the position of office manager. There are some things that I need to know about you, and then you can ask me some questions.

In general, the job requires expertise in the areas of accounting, administration of personnel forms, inventory records, payroll, and—other duties. How are you at making coffee?

INT:　I make great coffee, but I don't recall seeing that in the ad.

OWN:　You're right. Just a little joke. Ha, ha. Tell me, what do you see as your principal qualifications for the job?

INT:　Well, I have excellent typing and word processing skills—I've worked for five years in a similar position with another firm. I would, however, like to work in a smaller company. My duties in my previous job included payroll, bookkeeping, ordering supplies, and some supervision of office staff. I'm a quick learner, and believe that I would be an asset to your company.

OWN:　I'm sure you would be an asset. I asked before if you were married. Are you?

INT:　No, I've been divorced for three years.

OWN:　Any children?

INT:　Yes, two boys.

OWN: Well, then, how can I be sure that you'll be at work every day if you have to take care of them?

INT: I've arranged for day care, Mr. Winthrop—and I will be at work.

OWN: Is the day care near where you live?

INT: Yes, it's on Lincoln Street.

OWN: That's a pretty rough section of town, isn't it?

INT: Yes, but it's all I can afford right now.

OWN: Tell me, are you Hispanic or American Indian? I sometimes have trouble telling the difference.

INT: I'm Hispanic, but I don't see what that has to do with this job.

OWN: Now don't get touchy. I was just curious. I don't want any trouble with your people. By the way, do you have a car?

INT: No, why do you ask?

OWN: Well, I just want to make sure you can get to work.

INT: I *will* get to work, Mr. Winthrop.

OWN: And you don't have any handicaps or anything else I need to know about, do you? Health care costs are already sky high, and who knows what's going to happen now with the other party in the White House!

INT: No, I don't have any handicaps.

OWN: Well, Mrs. Ward, you seem qualified enough. I wasn't sure whether I would want a woman in this position, especially one who's still young enough to have children. But let me think about it. I'll get back to you in a few days.

INT: Thank you, Mr. Winthrop, but I thought you said I'd be able to ask questions.

OWN: Well, I've told you everything you need to know, and I'm out of time. I have a business to run, you know. Have a good day.

1. Identify the illegal or improper questions asked by Mr. Winthrop.
Explain your reasons for selecting each question. In your answer,
include your evaluation of the relevance of each question to Mrs.
Ward's ability to do a good job.

_____

_____

_____

_____

_____

_____

_____

_____

_____

_____

_____

_____

_____

_____

_____

_____

_____

_____

_____

_____

_____

2. Did any of Mrs. Ward's statements and/or actions seem inappropriate? Explain.

_____

_____

_____

_____

_____

_____

_____

_____

_____

_____

_____

3. If you were Mrs. Ward, how would you have responded to this interview? What options do you think you would have?

_____

_____

_____

_____

_____

_____

_____

_____

_____

_____

_____

Chapter 17: Operations and Staffing
Three Strikes and You're Out!

In Chapter 17, the three C's of credit were identified as character, capacity, and capital. Each of the following statements addresses one of these. Identify which by writing the correct term in the space provided to the left of each sentence.

_____   **1.** The applicant owns three homes.

_____   **2.** The applicant filed for bankruptcy one month ago.

_____   **3.** The applicant has a large savings account.

_____   **4.** A credit check on the applicant reveals several delinquent accounts.

_____   **5.** The applicant has been unemployed for six months.

_____   **6.** A business contacts the credit bureau regarding all new applications for credit.

_____   **7.** The applicant's monthly bills equal 50 percent of his/her monthly income.

_____   **8.** The applicant has a large stock portfolio.

_____   **9.** The applicant has no previous credit history.

_____   **10.** The applicant collects classic cars.

_____   **11.** The applicant has a half dozen credit cards and charge accounts and keeps payments current on all of them.

_____   **12.** The applicant is making monthly payments on a number of large loans—education, new car, condominium mortgage, and personal.

_____   **13.** The applicant has reached the credit limits on all of his or her bank cards and charge accounts.

_____   **14.** The applicant's assets are limited to an older model car and a small checking account.

_____   **15.** The applicant has a credit history that goes back more than 15 years.

_____   **16.** The applicant works two jobs.

Chapter 17: Operations and Staffing
Pin the Tail on the...?

It's time for a game. The object is to pin the right position on the blocks of a business's organization chart. *Hint:* It will help if you first decide which jobs are line positions and which are staff. This will narrow the number of potential placements for some of them.

In the box below is a list of the positions you have to work with. Unless otherwise indicated (by a number in parentheses), there is only one of each. Check them off as you place them in the chart.

Accountant

Advertising Specialist

Customer Service Representative

Manager

Office Manager

Owner

Purchasing Agent

Receptionist

Sales Manager

Sales Representatives (3)

Secretaries (3)

Shipping Clerk

Warehouse Manager

---

1. Distribute the named personnel in the organization chart on the facing page. As you work, remember organization chart conventions (like the significance of solid and broken lines). Start pinning!

2. Explain how you decided which positions were line personnel and which were staff. Refer to the chapter definitions of these terms to justify your answers.

_____

_____

_____

_____

_____

_____

_____

3. How would this chart be helpful to a manager working in the business?

_____

_____

_____

_____

_____

_____

_____

4. How would this chart be useful to other employees of the business?

_____

_____

_____

_____

_____

_____

_____

Chapter 18: Promoting Your Business

Cheaper Isn't Always Better

When trying to get the most for your advertising dollar, you can't always rely on obvious or readily available figures. For example, the newspaper with the largest circulation is not necessarily your best choice. Neither is the radio or television station with the lowest cost per ad. What you need to look at is the cost of reaching *your particular customers*.

The examples on this and the following page will guide you through the steps in this calculation. Generally, you must determine what portion of the particular medium's audience or circulation your customers represent and then divide the cost of the ad by this figure. Try it!

1. You are trying to decide between two local newspapers to advertise your product. The *Register* has a circulation of 50,000 and charges $1,500 for a quarter-page ad. The *Times* has a circulation of 45,000 and charges $1,600 for the same space. From your research you estimate that 30 percent of *Register* readers and 42 percent of *Times* readers are potential buyers of your product. Determine which paper offers the lower cost per potential customer.

	Register	Times
Circulation	_____	_____
Percentage of potential customers reached	_____	_____
Number of potential customers reached	_____	_____
Cost of ad	_____	_____
Cost of ad per reader	_____	_____
Cost of ad per potential customer reached	_____	_____
Paper with the lower cost per reader	_____	_____
Paper with the lower cost per potential customer (check one)	_____	_____

Chapter 18: Promoting Your Business

So What Can You Do with the Ghost of Christmas Past?

The head of the local theater company has just learned that you are becoming an expert in the development and management of small business ventures—specifically, the development and implementation of promotional plans. And has she got a deal for you!

The company is doing a production of *A Christmas Carol*. It will be presented on the weekends between Thanksgiving and Christmas. There will be evening performances on Fridays and Saturdays, with special children's matinees on Saturday afternoons. The children's performances will include refreshments and chaperons so that parents can "drop the kids off for a few hours" while they do their holiday shopping.

Your mission is to develop a dynamite promotional plan for the children's performances, one sure to fill the house and rattle the chains of Old Ebenezer himself. Use the questions spread over the next several pages to develop your ideas.

Planning

1. Who is your target market(s)?

   _____

   _____

2. Why should you refocus on your target market before selecting your promotional activities?

   _____

   _____

3. What is the theme you will present or the image that will guide your promotional efforts?

   _____

   _____

   _____

4. When will you begin to implement your promotional plan?

   _____

   _____

   _____

Selecting Your Promotional Mix

1. Based on your product (special matinees for children) and your market, which promotional channel(s) will you use? Explain.

_____

_____

_____

_____

_____

_____

_____

_____

2. Which element of the promotional mix will you use most? Why? What specific strategies will you use? Why?

_____

_____

_____

_____

_____

_____

_____

_____

_____

_____

Entrepreneurship and Small Business Management **119**

Name _____ Date _____

Publicity

 Develop a publicity release for the local newspaper. Use your own creativity and the following outline.

1. Who?

_____

_____

_____

_____

2. What?

_____

_____

_____

_____

3. Where?

_____

_____

_____

_____

4. When?

_____

_____

_____

_____

5. Why?

_____

_____

_____

_____

Advertising

Assuming that you selected radio as a medium in the advertising element of your promotional mix—and even if you didn't—develop a 30-second radio ad. To construct a successful radio ad, you should do the following:

- Grab the listener's attention—not only with words but with sound and music as well. (Describe how you would use sound effects and/or music.)
- Tell immediately what the benefit of the product is.
- Be sure to mention the name of the product often.
- Be positive, keep it simple, and speak in a conversational style.

_____

_____

_____

_____

_____

_____

_____

_____

_____

_____

_____

_____

_____

_____

_____

_____

_____

_____

_____

Sales Promotion

Sales promotion involves the use of incentives or interest-building activities to stimulate traffic or sales. Design a promotion to stimulate the sale of matinee tickets. In your description, be sure to include the type of promotion, a description, and your rationale as to why it will be effective. Be creative and provide as much detail as you can.

_____

_____

_____

_____

_____

_____

_____

_____

_____

_____

_____

_____

_____

_____

_____

_____

_____

_____

_____

_____

_____

Chapter 19: Record Keeping

The Check Is in the Mail

An important part of record keeping is keeping track of how much cash you have on hand. This is done by reconciling the monthly statement that you receive from the bank for your business's checking account. The reconciliation process is the same as that used for a personal checking account. The numbers may just be a little larger.

Below is a summary of the information from a checking account statement and register (the handwritten record you keep of the checks you write and the deposits you make). Use the reconciliation form on the following page to find out if your check register and bank statement are in agreement. (In other words, do your checkbook and bank statement balances match?)

Bank/Statement Balance

$1,875.92

Outstanding Checks

#1803	$ 5.39
1833	6.88
1851	25.73
1858	10.18
1863	125.73
1864	98.08
1869	327.33
1870	15.66
1871	32.93
1872	18.92
1873	6.57
1874	808.72

Outstanding Deposits

$ 319.57
1,429.38
319.57

Interest Earned

$ 32.73

Service Charges

$ 22.17

Account/Register Balance

$2,472.88

Name _____ Date _____

Bank Reconciliation Worksheet

ITEMS OUTSTANDING		
NUMBER	AMOUNT	
TOTAL	$	

TO BALANCE YOUR ACCOUNT:

ENTER
the new balance shown on
your statement. . . . . $_____

ADD
any deposits listed in your $_____
register that are not shown $_____
on your statement. $_____
                                              + $_____

                        TOTAL . . . . + $_____

CALCULATE THE SUBTOTAL. . . . . $_____

SUBTRACT
the total outstanding checks
and withdrawals from the
chart at left. . . . . − $_____

CALCULATE THE ENDING BALANCE
which should be the same as
the current balance in your
check register. . . . . $_____

Chapter 19: Record Keeping

Aging Without Growing Older

Keeping track of what clients owe you is known as aging accounts receivable. By aging your accounts receivable, you can determine who is slow in paying and who pays promptly. When using a manual system, the best way to do this is by setting up an aging table.

It is June 30, and you are getting ready to age your accounts receivable. Listed below are your clients, the date an invoice was generated, and the amount of the invoice. Using the table on the next page, mark the amount owed by each customer in the appropriate column. Then total the amounts due by "age" for your final answers. *Note:* In this business, an invoice is due 30 days from the date of its issuance.

Client	Date of Invoice	Amount of Invoice
A	May 28	$ 63.57
B	April 17	22.15
C	March 10	92.18
D	January 5	57.63
E	April 20	117.32
F	May 3	15.16
G	April 23	19.83
H	May 15	25.00
I	April 6	32.93
J	February 3	56.65
K	June 15	67.50
L	January 29	88.98
M	March 16	93.73
N	April 18	17.62
O	March 20	31.93
P	May 20	87.20
Q	February 20	76.30
R	April 2	91.73
S	March 3	18.20
T	June 2	27.63
U	May 21	32.90
V	March 11	41.73
W	April 16	48.23
X	January 20	56.30
Y	March 14	11.25
Z	June 14	70.63

Client	Not due	1–30 days past due	31–60 days past due	61–90 days past due	Over 90 days past due
A					
B					
C					
D					
E					
F					
G					
H					
I					
J					
K					
L					
M					
N					
O					
P					
Q					
R					
S					
T					
U					
V					
W					
X					
Y					
Z					
Total					
Percent of Total					

Chapter 20: Financing Your Business
Wanted: Pennies from Heaven

How much money will you need to start a business? How much money do you have? Where will you find money? How will you be evaluated by a banker?

All of these questions must be answered as you prepare to finance your business. Chapter 20 points out that the main source of start-up capital for new businesses is an entrepreneur's own personal savings. If this is the case, then you need to spend some time analyzing your personal financial position.

Even if you decide to seek potential investors or go to a bank, the lender will be interested in studying your financial condition. Below is an example of a very simple personal financial statement prepared for this purpose. Notice that it follows the basic format of a balance sheet in that total assets equal total liabilities plus net worth (the personal equivalent of owner's equity).

The next two pages contain a much more complex personal financial statement. Complete as much of it as you can. Since the two-page form is so comprehensive, you may find yourself unable to complete many of its entries. You can probably use it, however, to construct your own statement, one that falls midway between the two extremes presented here.

Personal Financial Statement

Steven J. Kent
Statement of Financial Condition
August 23, 19– –

Assets

Cash in checking accounts	$1,200	
Cash in savings accounts	5,000	
Personal property and furnishings	850	
Total Assets		$7,050

Liabilities

Short-term loans	$ 500	
Miscellaneous charge accounts	300	
Truck loan	5,000	
Total Liabilities		5,800

Net Worth

Steven J. Kent		$1,250

Name _____ Date _____

PERSONAL FINANCIAL STATEMENT

Financial Statement as of _____ 19_____. If you are seeking credit jointly with your spouse, or if you are relying on your spouse's assets or income in requesting credit, this statement should reflect the financial condition of your spouse as well as your own financial condition.

APPLICANT'S NAME	DATE OF BIRTH	CO-APPLICANT (INCLUDES APPLICANT'S SPOUSE)	DATE OF BIRTH
RESIDENCE ADDRESS		RELATIONSHIP TO APPLICANT	
		RESIDENCE ADDRESS	
EMPLOYED BY		EMPLOYED BY	

BUSINESS ADDRESS	TELEPHONE NO.	BUSINESS ADDRESS	TELEPHONE NO.
KIND OF BUSINESS / POSITION	HOW LONG THERE	KIND OF BUSINESS / POSITION	HOW LONG THERE

FIXED OR AVERAGE SALARY $ PER	Income you may receive from alimony, child support, or maintenance payments need not be revealed if you do not choose to disclose such income in applying for credit	FIXED OR AVERAGE SALARY $ PER	Income you may receive from alimony, child support, or maintenance payments need not be revealed if you do not choose to disclose such income in applying for credit
AMOUNT OF OTHER INCOME $	SOURCE — RENTALS, DIVIDENDS, ETC.	AMOUNT OF OTHER INCOME $	SOURCE — RENTALS, DIVIDENDS, ETC.

NAME OF BANK WHERE YOU DEPOSIT	BRANCH		SAVINGS	CHECKING

ASSETS		IN EVEN DOLLARS		LIABILITIES		IN EVEN DOLLARS	
CASH ON HAND & IN BANKS				NOTES PAYABLE TO BANKS	(SCHED. D)		
MARKETABLE SECURITIES	(SCHED. A)			NOTES PAYABLE TO OTHERS	(SCHED. D)		
NON-MARKETABLE SECURITIES	(SCHED. B)			ACCOUNTS PAYABLE	(SCHED. E)		
RESTRICTED OR CONTROL STOCK	(SCHED. B)			REAL ESTATE MORTGAGES	(SCHED. F)		
SECURITIES HELD BY BROKERS IN MARGIN ACCTS.				DUE TO BROKERS			
REAL ESTATE	(SCHED. F)			UNPAID INCOME TAX			
NOTES RECEIVABLE	(SCHED. G)			CREDIT CARDS (OUTSTANDING BALANCE)			
ACCOUNTS RECEIVABLE	(SCHED. G)			OTHER LIABILITIES (ITEMIZE)			
CASH VALUE—LIFE INSURANCE	(SCHED. C)						
AUTOS YEAR MAKE							
YEAR MAKE							
HOUSEHOLD GOODS							
JEWELRY							
ASSETS HELD IN TRUST							
OTHER ASSETS (ITEMIZE)				(SEE SCHEDULE H FOR CONTINGENT LIAB.)			
				TOTAL LIABILITIES			
				NET WORTH			
TOTAL ASSETS				TOTAL LIABILITIES AND NET WORTH			

DETAILS RELATIVE TO ASSETS AND LIABILITIES (IF SPACE IS INSUFFICIENT, ATTACH SUPPLEMENTAL LIST)

(A) MARKETABLE SECURITIES—LIST	TITLE IN NAME OF	PREF. OR COMMON	NO. OF SHARES	MARKET VALUE	SHARES PLEDGED	WHERE PLEDGED

The Ohio laws against discrimination require that all creditors make credit equally available to all creditworthy customers, and that credit reporting agencies maintain separate credit histories on each individual upon request. The Ohio Civil Rights Commission administers compliance with this law.

This financial statement is submitted for the purpose of procuring, establishing and maintaining credit with you in behalf of the undersigned or persons, firms or corporations in whose behalf the undersigned may either severally or jointly with others execute a guaranty in your favor. The undersigned warrants that this financial statement is true and correct and authorizes the Bank to obtain information concerning any statements made herein.

DATE THIS STATEMENT SIGNED: _____ SIGNED: _____

DATE THIS STATEMENT SIGNED: _____ SIGNED: _____

Copyright © Glencoe, Macmillan/McGraw-Hill

(B) NON-MARKETABLE SECURITIES—LIST (INCLUDING RESTRICTED OR CONTROL STOCK)	TITLE IN NAME OF	SHARES OWNED	SHARES ISSUED	BOOK OR OTHER VALUE	SHARES PLEDGED	WHERE PLEDGED

(C) LIFE INSURANCE COMPANY	OWNER	FACE AMOUNT	BENEFICIARY	KIND OF INSURANCE	CASH VALUE	AMOUNT OF POLICY LOAN

(D) NOTES PAYABLE—TO	AMOUNT	DATE MADE	DATE DUE	REPAYMENT SCHEDULE	SECURED OR ENDORSED BY

(E) ACCOUNTS PAYABLE—TO	AMOUNT	DATE MADE	DATE DUE	FOR WHAT

(F) REAL ESTATE—DESCRIPTION	LOCATION	TITLE IN WHOSE NAME	AMOUNT OF INSURANCE
1.			
2.			
3.			
4.			
5.			
6.			

DATE ACQUIRED	ORIGINAL COST	1ST MORTGAGE BALANCE	2ND MORTGAGE BALANCE	1ST MORTGAGE PAYMENT	2ND MORTGAGE PAYMENT	REAL ESTATE TAXES	RENTALS REC'D DURING LAST CALENDAR YEAR
1.							
2.							
3.							
4.							
5.							
6.							

MORTGAGE HOLDERS—FIRST MORTGAGE HELD BY	SECOND MORTGAGE HELD BY
PARCEL NO. 1	
PARCEL NO. 2	
PARCEL NO. 3	
PARCEL NO. 4	
PARCEL NO. 5	
PARCEL NO. 6	

(G) ACCTS. & NOTES RECEIVABLE—FROM	AMT. DUE	MATURITY	REPAYMENT SCHEDULE	SECURITY—IF ANY

(H) CONTINGENT LIABILITIES	(DEBTOR)	AMOUNT
AS ENDORSER, CO-MAKER OR GUARANTOR		
ON LEASES OR CONTRACTS		
OTHER		

REMARKS

Chapter 20: Financing Your Business

Business Proposal Assessment

For the last ten chapters, you have been collecting information for your business plan. Now you must take all of the information you have gathered and make some sense of it. The Business Proposal Assessment that appears on the next several pages can help. It asks many of the tough questions that you must answer before you can develop an effective business plan.

Take a look at the plan to see how it is organized. Fill out as much information as you can and think about how you want to present your business to potential investors, partners, and employees. Refer back to previous activities and chapters for ideas. Remember, this is a draft, so there are no right or wrong answers. However, you may want to schedule an appointment with a professional (lender, SBA representative, SBDC counselor) for advice and tips on how to improve your plan. Good luck!

The Ohio Small Business Development Center
Business Proposal Assessment   **BUSINESS PLAN GUIDE**

Please complete this questionnaire and have it available when you meet with the SBDC Counselor. Attach additional sheets as needed.

Name: _____
Company Name (if known): _____
Address: _____
Phone: (_____) _____

1. Describe the product/service you are planning to offer in your business. Be sure to include specifically what the product/service will do for your customers, the methods or technologies to be used, the business location, and the geographic area to be served.
   (**For a Product:** Specify if manufacturing or other, business or consumer market, etc.)
   (**For a Service:** Specify the type of service, i.e., retailing, a business or a consumer service, etc.)
   Describe product/service: _____
   _____
   _____
   _____
   _____

2. Is this business ...
   [ ] A new business   [ ] An expansion of a current business   [ ] A take-over of an existing business
   [ ] Other type of business [DESCRIBE] _____
   [ ] Not sure what business will be

3. Is your business going to be a ...
   [ ] Sole Proprietorship   [ ] Corporation
   [ ] Partnership—Who will your partners be? _____
   [ ] Other type of business [DESCRIBE] _____
   [ ] Not sure what type business will be

---

4. Why are you going into this business? Think about your financial and non-financial goals.

Financial goals: _____

_____

_____

Non-financial goals: _____

_____

_____

I. Marketing Issues

5. Who is your target market (i.e., potential customers)? For consumer products/services, be sure to include general demographic information (such as age, income, gender, etc.) and behavior characteristics (such as life-styles, opinions, etc.). For business products/services, include the business classifications or descriptions and the size of the business you will serve.

_____

_____

_____

6. Describe your target market's buying habits. Think about information such as seasonal/cyclical demand patterns, frequency of purchase, competitive contracts, customized contracts or price lists, etc.

_____

_____

_____

_____

7. Describe your primary competitors (include names and locations, sales patterns, etc.) and explain a little bit about how well their businesses are doing. Also explain a little about the industry and any relevant changes within the industry.

_____

_____

_____

_____

8. Why do you think customers will buy from you? (Include product/service benefits, strengths, weaknesses, as well as operational and marketable differences between your product/service and competitors' products/services.)

_____

_____

_____

_____

9. Describe the size of the current market and about what percent of the market you think you may get. Think about the market's historic (last 3–5 years) and future (next 2–3 years) growth rate.

_____

_____

_____

_____

10. Describe your future new markets (such as geographic locations, new customers, etc.) or new products (additions to the line or new lines).

_____

_____

_____

_____

33. How much will you need in total to start your business? $ _____

34. About what percent of this money will come from ...

Personal funds   _____ %
Borrow from family   _____ %
Borrow from bank   _____ %
Seek private investors _____ %
        TOTAL   100   %

35. Explain specifically what this money will be used for?

_____
_____
_____
_____
_____

36. What assets are you willing to use as collateral against money you are borrowing? Be sure to speak with anyone who may also be affected by you using this as collateral.
[ ] Nothing
[ ] House or personal real estate
[ ] Car
[ ] Other [SPECIFY] _____

37. Are you willing to give up ownership rights in the company or share ownership?
[ ] Yes
[ ] Would definitely prefer not to, but would if required
[ ] No

38. Who will be responsible for your debts (i.e., co-signer) if the business fails? Be sure you have consulted with this person.

_____
_____
_____
_____
_____

Chapter 21: Managing Your Operation

"I'm So Busy—I Never Get Anything Done!"

How well do you manage your time? How often do you hear someone say, "I really want to do that, but I don't have any time." Are you one of those people? Well, let's see how you spend your time. And let's find out if you are spending it doing the things that will help you get where you want to go. That is really all that time management is—managing time so you can achieve what you want to achieve (even if it's to sleep in on Saturday morning).

Activity 1

First, ask yourself how you spend your time. Use the chart on page 136 to record how many hours a day you *think* you spend on a given activity. Some categories of activities are listed for you. Use an additional sheet of paper if you have more activities to list than there is room for in each box. (You can design your own grid if you wish.) Complete this first chart before moving on to the next activity.

Activity 2

So, now you have a chart of how you think you spend your time. But wait! Does it represent the best use you can make of your time? Think—how would you spend your time if you wanted to do your utmost to accomplish your goals? Summarize your conclusions by filling in the chart on page 137. (*Note:* You may need to take a few minutes to consider what your goals are before you begin—educational, social, personal, career, and so on.) Complete this second chart before moving on to the next activity.

Activity 3

Now it's time to find out how you actually spend your time. For one week, keep a daily record of every activity you engage in and the amount of time you spend on it. At the end of each day, summarize your data by making appropriate entries in the chart that appears on page 138.

Activity 4

At week's end, you will have three charts—one showing how you think you spend your time, another showing how you could most effectively spend your time, and a third showing how you actually spend your time. When you have these three charts completed, you will be ready to answer the questions that begin on page 139.

Name _____ Date _____

Chart 1—How You Think You Spend Your Time

	Sun.	Mon.	Tues.	Wed.	Thurs.	Fri.	Sat.
Sleeping							
Eating							
Classes							
Homework							
Hygiene							
Athletics							
Daydreaming							
Social time							
Bus/car rides							
Shopping							
Chores							
Reading (leisure)							
Church							
Other activities							

Name _____ Date _____

Chart 2—How You Could Spend Your Time Most Effectively

	Sun.	Mon.	Tues.	Wed.	Thurs.	Fri.	Sat.
Sleeping							
Eating							
Classes							
Homework							
Hygiene							
Athletics							
Daydreaming							
Social time							
Bus/car rides							
Shopping							
Chores							
Reading (leisure)							
Church							
Other activities							

Name _____ Date _____

Chart 3—How You Actually Spend Your Time

	Sun.	Mon.	Tues.	Wed.	Thurs.	Fri.	Sat.
Sleeping							
Eating							
Classes							
Homework							
Hygiene							
Athletics							
Daydreaming							
Social time							
Bus/car rides							
Shopping							
Chores							
Reading (leisure)							
Church							
Other activities							

1. After comparing the three charts, what did you discover that came as a surprise?

_____

_____

_____

_____

_____

_____

2. What are the major differences between how you think you spend your time (Chart 1) and how you actually spend it (Chart 3)?

_____

_____

_____

_____

_____

_____

3. What are the major differences between how you believe you should spend your time (Chart 2) and how you actually spend it (Chart 3)?

_____

_____

_____

_____

_____

_____

4. What changes will you need to make in your schedule in order to make more time for the activities in Chart 2?

_____

_____

_____

_____

_____

_____

_____

_____

_____

5. Do you believe you are managing your time well? If not, what short- and long-term goals could you consider to manage your time better? If you are managing your time well, are there changes you might make to fine-tune your use of time? If so, describe them.

_____

_____

_____

_____

_____

_____

_____

_____

_____

_____

_____

_____

Chapter 21: Managing Your Operation

O Captain, My Captain

This story is, in a way, an example of management at its best and its worst in a particular situation. While it is obviously not a business story, you are going to apply some of the key points from Chapter 21 to assess the captain's management style and effectiveness.

On the next three pages are questions about this story. Be sure to relate each response to actual business management as it was discussed in the chapter.

Two battleships assigned to the training squadron had been at sea on maneuvers in heavy weather for several days. I was serving on the lead battleship and was on watch on the bridge as night fell. The visibility was poor with patchy fog, so the captain remained on the bridge keeping an eye on all activities.

Shortly after dark, the lookout on the wing of the bridge reported, "Light, bearing on the starboard bow."

"Is it steady or moving astern?" the captain called out.

Lookout replied, "Steady, captain," which meant we were on a dangerous collision course with that ship.

The captain then called to the signalman, "Signal that ship: We are on a collision course, advise you change course 20 degrees."

Back came a signal, "Advisable for you to change course 20 degrees."

The captain said, "Send, I'm a captain, change course 20 degrees."

"I'm a seaman second class," came the reply. "You had better change course 20 degrees."

By that time, the captain was furious. He spat out, "Send, I'm a battleship. Change course 20 degrees."

Back came the flashing light, "I'm a lighthouse."

We changed course.

From *Proceedings*, the magazine of the Naval Institute.

1. Using the four management functions (planning, organizing, directing, and controlling), explain how the captain of the battleship was an effective manager.

   a. Planning:

   _____

   _____

   _____

   _____

   _____

   _____

b. Organizing:

_____

_____

_____

_____

_____

_____

_____

c. Directing:

_____

_____

_____

_____

_____

_____

_____

d. Controlling:

_____

_____

_____

_____

_____

_____

_____

2. How would you describe the captain's leadership style in this situation? Explain your choice.

_____

_____

_____

_____

_____

_____

_____

_____

_____

_____

3. Would you say this is an example of situational management? If so, why?

_____

_____

_____

_____

_____

_____

_____

_____

_____

_____

_____

_____

MARIO'S ITALIAN RESTAURANT
Purchase Order

Vendor: B   *Purchase Order No.:* 2002

Qty.	Description	Unit Cost	Total

Total Amount _____

Shipping _____

Total due _____

MARIO'S ITALIAN RESTAURANT
Purchase Order

Vendor: C   *Purchase Order No.:* 2003

Qty.	Description	Unit Cost	Total

Total Amount _____

Shipping _____

Total due _____

MARIO'S ITALIAN RESTAURANT
Purchase Order

Vendor: D   *Purchase Order No.:* 2004

Qty.	Description	Unit Cost	Total

Total Amount _____

Shipping _____

Total due _____

---

2. What is the actual price per pound of pasta from each vendor when discounts are calculated and delivery charges are included? (Round to the nearest cent.)

   A. _____

   B. _____

   C. _____

   D. _____

3. Which vendor should Mario choose?

   _____

   _____

   _____

4. The chapter suggests that you should not give all of your business to one vendor. If Mario were to buy 70 percent of his pasta from one vendor and 30 percent from another vendor, which two vendors should he choose for the lowest combined price? (Assume he's buying 100 pounds and don't forget shipping charges.) Is this amount lower or higher than buying from the vendor chosen in question 3?

_____

_____

_____

_____

_____

_____

_____

_____

_____

5. Are there other variables that Mario might consider in making his decision that are not included in the information given? Name them and explain their importance.

_____

_____

_____

_____

_____

_____

_____

_____

_____

_____

Chapter 22: Purchasing, Inventory, and Production Management

Good Old George

Old George is a pretty fair mechanic down in Ohmagosh, but he is tight with his money. There is a story that might explain why.

Some years ago George heard there was going to be a shortage of engine blocks due to a union disagreement at a major manufacturer. Since George did a large business in rebuilt engines at the local raceway, he doubled his normal inventory. In order to accomplish this, he got a loan from the local bank. This meant that George now was living on a very tight profit margin. But he figured when the shortage hit, the number of customers would increase substantially, and he'd really make out then.

Now, he also had problems storing the engines. Since his garage was not very big, he had to put some in a back room. He was a bit concerned about security, but he had never had trouble before.

One month following the purchase and delivery of the engine blocks, the raceway announced that it would be closing. George could not believe his ears. He was ruined!

Years later, George is still fixing engines, but he demands cash up front before he will order a part. It wasn't too long ago that he sold (practically gave) the last of those engines to a neighborhood kid restoring an old car. Yep, old George is tight with a dollar down in Ohmagosh.

1. What mistakes do you think George made that led to his loss?

_____

_____

_____

_____

_____

_____

_____

_____

_____

_____

_____

_____

2. In Chapter 22, the section on inventory management lists six costs associated with too much inventory. Describe those that relate to George's decision and result.

_____

_____

_____

_____

_____

_____

_____

3. What might George have done differently in order to have minimized his risk in this situation?

_____

_____

_____

_____

_____

_____

_____

4. What did you learn from George that will be helpful to you as you manage inventory for your business?

_____

_____

_____

_____

_____

_____

_____

Chapter 23: Human Resource Management

XYZ—PDQ

In the section "How Managers Influence Motivation," Douglas McGregor's Theory X and Theory Y were discussed. You are now going to do your own research to discover how people around you think.

Using the questionnaire below, interview 15 people and record their responses. Mark 5 if they strongly agree, 1 if they strongly disagree, or some number in between. Try to be as accurate as possible. After you collect all the data from the questionnaires, assess the interviewees' potential as future managers based on the questions that follow the questionnaire.

	Strongly Agree				Strongly Disagree
1. People do not like work and try to avoid it.	5	4	3	2	1
2. Managers have to push people, closely supervise them, or threaten them with punishment to get them to produce.	5	4	3	2	1
3. People have little or no ambition and will try to avoid responsibility.	5	4	3	2	1
4. Work is natural to people and is actually an important part of their lives.	5	4	3	2	1
5. People will work toward goals if they are committed to them.	5	4	3	2	1
6. People become committed to goals when it is clear that achieving them will bring personal rewards.	5	4	3	2	1
7. Under the right conditions, people not only accept responsibility but also seek it out.	5	4	3	2	1
8. People have a high degree of imagination, ingenuity, and creativity, all of which can be used in solving an organization's problems.	5	4	3	2	1
9. Employees have much more potential than organizations actually use.	5	4	3	2	1

1. Using your own judgment, how many of the 15 people interviewed would be good managers? What makes you think so? Do they tend to make Theory X or Theory Y assumptions?

_____

_____

_____

_____

_____

_____

_____

_____

2. Based on what you think makes a good manager, what would be the highest score an interviewee could attain? What would be the lowest? Show how you calculate this.

_____

_____

_____

_____

_____

_____

_____

_____

_____

_____

3. What did you learn about your interviewees' attitude concerning motivation?

_____

_____

_____

_____

_____

_____

_____

_____

_____

_____

4. Has your attitude about motivation changed after carrying out this questionnaire and reading the chapter? Do you agree or disagree with the authors that those who hold Theory Y assumptions make the best managers?

_____

_____

_____

_____

_____

_____

_____

_____

_____

_____

_____

_____

Chapter 23: Human Resource Management

Inside or Outside?

You are the owner of a small computer business, and one of your employees has just resigned. She filled an important management position in your company.

Several employees in the company might be able to fill the position. But you also know of three people who are currently working for competitors who might be interested in the position.

You must decide whether to recruit internally or externally. Your decision should take into consideration the positive and negative consequences of your decision.

1. What are the advantages of selecting someone from within the organization to fill the position? What are the disadvantages?

_____

_____

_____

_____

_____

_____

_____

_____

_____

_____

_____

_____

_____

_____

_____

_____

_____

_____

2. What are the advantages of selecting an employee from a competitor?
What are the disadvantages?

_____

_____

_____

_____

_____

_____

_____

_____

_____

_____

3. How would you decide?

_____

_____

_____

_____

_____

_____

_____

_____

_____

_____

Chapter 23: Human Resource Management

Is John Technophobic?

John had worked for a small PR firm for 15 years. He had held the same typesetting position for most of the time he had been employed there.

John was a good employee. He was rarely absent, came to work on time, did his job with little comment, and went home.

Recently, the firm began to update production and communication equipment. Many employees, including John, were having to learn new skills. John's incidents of absenteeism increased, and his overall job performance was noticeably lower than before. It seemed John was no longer as motivated as before.

1. What would you do to re-motivate John?

_____

_____

_____

_____

_____

_____

_____

_____

2. How would you keep him motivated?

_____

_____

_____

_____

_____

_____

_____

_____

_____

3. Can you think of anything that might have been done to prevent the change in John?

_____

_____

_____

_____

_____

_____

_____

_____

_____

_____

_____

Chapter 24: Financial Management

How Is Your Financial Health?

One of the ways businesses analyze their financial condition is to compare certain numbers from a balance sheet or income statement. This analysis to compare the relationship between the two figures is called ratio analysis.

Based on the guidelines presented in the chapter, calculate the following ratios and state what the ratio tells about the business. If you are unable to determine from the information given, write *Cannot determine*. (*Note:* Round to the second decimal place.)

1. Calculate the current ratio based on the following information:

Current assets	650,000
Current liabilities	400,000

Current ratio = _____

_____

_____

_____

_____

_____

2. Calculate the current ratio based on the following information:

Current assets	850,000
Current liabilities	325,000

Current ratio = _____

_____

_____

_____

_____

_____

Name _____ Date _____

1. What is the available cash for December?

_____

2. What is the ending cash balance as of December 31?

_____

3. Why is Simone unhappy?

_____

_____

_____

_____

_____

_____

_____

_____

_____

_____

_____

_____

_____

_____

_____

_____

_____

_____

4. What should Simone do to manage her pending cash flow difficulty? What does she need to do to lessen the possibility that this situation will reoccur?

_____

_____

_____

_____

_____

_____

_____

_____

_____

_____

_____

Chapter 25: Computers in Small Business Management

What Can Computers Do for You?

The small business you hope to have one day may need to be computerized. Even a business that is reasonably well organized will benefit from computerization if it has large amounts of detailed information that need to be handled with speed and accuracy.

You will need to know how a computer can help you conduct your business better. Below, describe how each of the following business operations would be hampered if done manually. In other words, if you decided not to computerize, what problems might result?

1. Accounting

_____

_____

_____

_____

2. Advertising

_____

_____

_____

_____

_____

3. Inventory

_____

_____

_____

_____

_____

4. Payroll

_____

_____

_____

_____

5. Planning

_____

_____

_____

_____

6. Filing

_____

_____

_____

_____

7. Correspondence

_____

_____

_____

_____

8. Shipping and Receiving

_____

_____

_____

_____

Name _____   Date _____

It's Like Riding a Bicycle!

Mildred and Joshua have been bicycle enthusiasts for years. Two years ago, they fulfilled a long-time goal and opened a bicycle sales and repair shop. They are doing so well that they are having difficulty keeping up with the "chains and gears" of the business. There are inventory records, accounts receivable and payable, payroll (they have two employees other than themselves), mailing lists of customers, vendor information, correspondence, sales data, product information, financial records, credit information, and plans and ideas for the future of their business.

Mildred thinks they need to look into a computer. Joshua has finally agreed, although he is uncertain since no one in the shop can use a computer. Another drawback is that they have limited resources and are not sure that they can afford a major capital outlay.

They need to make a decision and are looking to you for advice. What do they need to do?

1. List all of the activities performed by the business that might be computerized.

   A. _____

   B. _____

   C. _____

   D. _____

   E. _____

   F. _____

   G. _____

   H. _____

   I. _____

   J. _____

   K. _____

   L. _____

2. Prioritize the activities you listed. Put those that most need to be computerized first at the top of the list and those that least need to be computerized at the bottom.

A. _____

B. _____

C. _____

D. _____

E. _____

F. _____

G. _____

H. _____

I. _____

J. _____

K. _____

L. _____

3. For each task to be computerized, figure out what information is needed and in what form (refer to the chapter if you need some help).

A. _____

_____

_____

_____

_____

B. _____

_____

_____

_____

_____

Name _____ Date _____

C. _____
_____
_____

D. _____
_____
_____

E. _____
_____
_____

F. _____
_____
_____

G. _____
_____
_____

H. _____
_____
_____

I. _____
_____
_____

J. _____
_____
_____
_____

K. _____

_____

_____

_____

L. _____

_____

_____

_____

4. Determine which general types of software Mildred and Joshua
   might need.

_____

_____

_____

_____

5. What advice would you give Mildred and Joshua about a computer
   system (in-house, bureau, time sharing)? Explain your reasons including
   why they shouldn't choose the other options.

_____

_____

_____

_____

_____

_____

_____

_____

Chapter 26: Marketing Management

Bad News Bears?

You can't assume that the target markets, customer demands, and competition you identify in starting up your business will remain the same. Just ask the big bear sellers. Review the facts from the case below and help the bewildered bear bunch with their marketing planning.

Business was great when we first started. My wife had been making these monogrammed stuffed bears as a hobby. Then she began selling them to people to give as gifts. Pretty soon we had a little plant set up with employees and all, and we were selling to stores all over the state. It seemed that as long as we could turn out stuffed bears, people would buy them.

Then all of a sudden, sales took a nose dive. We had no idea why.

Up until then, we had been doing most of our selling by sending catalogs to potential outlets. But with sales in such bad shape, I thought I had better get out on the road and call on our customers in person.

It didn't take long to find out the problem. Almost every store I went into had somebody else's bears—different designs and shapes, but bears just the same. On top of everything else, they were lower priced.

Well, we were able to get back some of our customers by giving bigger discounts, but it really cut into our profits. Now we have to figure out how to get the business back where it was. There are lots of questions we're going to have to answer.

1. How can the bear makers find out what customers want now?

_____

_____

_____

_____

_____

_____

_____

_____

_____

_____

_____

2. How can the bear makers make prices competitive and still make a profit?

_____

_____

_____

_____

_____

_____

_____

_____

_____

3. Is there a better way to distribute the products?

_____

_____

_____

_____

_____

_____

_____

_____

_____

_____

4. Is there a better way to sell the bears?

_____

_____

_____

_____

_____

_____

_____

_____

_____

_____

_____

_____

_____

_____

_____

_____

_____

_____

_____

_____

_____

_____

5. What have you learned about the need for revising your marketing plan?

_____

_____

_____

_____

_____

_____

_____

_____

_____

_____

_____

_____

_____

_____

_____

_____

_____

_____

_____

_____

_____

_____

Chapter 27: Social and Ethical Responsibility

Who Foots the Bill?

Nicholas is an 18-year-old senior in high school. He lives at home, and his sole source of income for the past year has been delivering papers and mowing lawns. In January, just after his birthday, he received an unsolicited credit card application from a new electronics store that is targeting young consumers in a special promotion. The business is trying to establish loyalty among young people as they enter the work force. The letter stated that he was preapproved for a card with a $1,000 limit. All he had to do was fill out, sign, and return the credit application.

Four weeks later, Nicholas received a new credit card with a $1,000 limit. With this new-found purchasing power, he bought some new stereo components and a watch for his girlfriend. The total charges were over $900.

At the end of February, he received his first statement detailing purchases and the minimum amount now owed. He didn't have enough money to pay the bill so he just threw it away. This continued for three months until the store threatened legal action to force Nicholas to pay the bill.

1. How would you assess the ethical behavior of the business in granting credit to Nicholas? Explain.

_____

_____

_____

_____

_____

_____

_____

2. How would you assess the ethical behavior of Nicholas in this situation? Explain.

_____

_____

_____

_____

_____

_____

_____

3. How would you advise Ms. Guzman?

_____

_____

_____

_____

_____

_____

4. What would you do if you were one of Ms. Guzman's customers, your profit margin was narrow, and her prices went up?

_____

_____

_____

_____

_____

_____

5. How could Ms. Guzman most effectively market this change? Give specific examples of strategies and activities that might support the strategies.

_____

_____

_____

_____

_____

_____

2. Chapter 28 identifies and defines market penetration as a type of intensive growth strategy. Explain how Stew Leonard used market penetration in the growth of his business. Provide specific examples in your explanation.

_____

_____

_____

_____

_____

_____

_____

_____

3. Chapter 28 identifies and defines product development as a type of intensive growth strategy. Explain how Stew Leonard used product development in the growth of his business. Provide specific examples in your explanation.

_____

_____

_____

_____

_____

_____

_____

_____

_____

4. Explain how Stew Leonard used forward integration as a strategy for growth. Be specific.

_____

_____

_____

_____

_____

_____

_____

_____

_____

_____

_____

5. Did Stew Leonard use synergistic diversification as a growth strategy? Explain.

_____

_____

_____

_____

_____

_____

_____

_____

_____

_____

_____

6. How important has the development of personnel at Stew Leonard's store been to the success of the business?

_____

_____

_____

_____

_____

_____

_____

_____

_____

7. What are some other ways Stew Leonard's maximized growth probability and minimized growth risks? You may go beyond the chapter explanations of growth to include your own analysis of Stew Leonard's success.

_____

_____

_____

_____

_____

_____

_____

_____

_____

_____

_____